Children and Computers

Elisa L. Klein, *Editor*

NEW DIRECTIONS FOR CHILD DEVELOPMENT
WILLIAM DAMON, *Editor-in-Chief*

Number 28, June 1985

Paperback sourcebooks in
The Jossey-Bass Social and Behavioral Sciences Series

Jossey-Bass Inc., Publishers
San Francisco • Washington • London

Elisa L. Klein (Ed.).
Children and Computers.
New Directions for Child Development, no. 28.
San Francisco: Jossey-Bass, 1985.

New Directions for Child Development Series
William Damon, *Editor-in-Chief*

New Directions for Child Development (publication number
USPS 494-090) is published quarterly by Jossey-Bass Inc., Publishers.
Second-class postage rates are paid at San Francisco, California,
and at additional mailing offices.

Correspondence:
Subscriptions, single-issue orders, change of address notices, undelivered
copies, and other correspondence should be sent to Subscriptions,
Jossey-Bass Inc., Publishers, 433 California Street, San Francisco,
California 94104.

Editorial correspondence should be sent to the Editor-in-Chief,
William Damon, Department of Psychology, Clark University,
Worcester, Massachusetts 01610.

Library of Congress Catalogue Card Number LC 84-82365
International Standard Serial Number ISSN 0195-2269
International Standard Book Number ISBN 7589-795-9

Cover art by Willi Baum
Manufactured in the United States of America

Ordering Information

The paperback sourcebooks listed below are published quarterly and can be ordered either by subscription or single-copy.

Subscriptions cost $35.00 per year for institutions, agencies, and libraries. Individuals can subscribe at the special rate of $25.00 per year *if payment is by personal check.* (Note that the full rate of $35.00 applies if payment is by institutional check, even if the subscription is designated for an individual.) Standing orders are accepted. Subscriptions normally begin with the first of the four sourcebooks in the current publication year of the series. When ordering, please indicate if you prefer your subscription to begin with the first issue of the *coming* year.

Single copies are available at $8.95 when payment accompanies order, and *all single-copy orders under $25.00 must include payment.* (California, New Jersey, New York, and Washington, D.C., residents please include appropriate sales tax.) For billed orders, cost per copy is $8.95 plus postage and handling. (Prices subject to change without notice.)

Bulk orders (ten or more copies) of any individual sourcebook are available at the following discounted prices: 10–49 copies, $8.05 each; 50–100 copies, $7.15 each; over 100 copies, *inquire.* Sales tax and postage and handling charges apply as for single copy orders.

To ensure correct and prompt delivery, all orders must give either the *name of an individual* or an *official purchase order number.* Please submit your order as follows:

Subscriptions: specify series and year subscription is to begin.
Single Copies: specify sourcebook code (such as, CD8) and first two words
of title.

Mail orders for United States and Possessions, Latin America, Canada, Japan, Australia, and New Zealand to:
Jossey-Bass Inc., Publishers
433 California Street
San Francisco, California 94104

Mail orders for all other parts of the world to:
Jossey-Bass Limited
28 Banner Street
London EC1Y 8QE

New Directions for Child Development Series
William Damon, *Editor-in-Chief*

Contents

Editor's Notes

The study of children's interactions with computers is a relatively recent phenomenon. Papert's (1980) assertion that the computer environment may enhance logical thought sparked much of the current research on the impact of the computer on children's cognitive development. This research was aided by the introduction of such computer languages as LOGO, such software as Bank Street Writer, and such peripherals as touch pads and light pens, which all eased the child's access to the computer. A casual glance at conference proceedings of the Society for Research in Child Development, the American Educational Research Association, and the Jean Piaget Society for the past few years reveals that interest in the role of computers in children's development and learning is increasing.

The purpose of this volume is to examine children's interactions with computers from a developmental perspective. Starting with early childhood and continuing through middle childhood, adolescence, and young adulthood, the contributors explore some of the fundamental assumptions about development and learning within the context of a highly technological environment.

In Chapter One, Christine Chaille and Barbara Littman discuss the importance of experience with the physical world during early childhood. The unique ability of computer simulations to represent and highlight critical information and relationships involved in natural phenomena may contribute to a more meaningful and useful understanding of how the physical world works. Chaille and Littman discuss how computer simulations are valuable extensions of the object-based activities found in many early childhood programs. Simulations give children greater access to and more control over the information in a problem, and thus they may help children to develop more accurate, useful ideas about natural phenomena.

In Chapter Two, George Forman offers a new definition for the type of symbol system used in computer graphics, kinetic print. Through computers, young children will be able to learn an "alphabet of movements" instead of an alphabet of static symbols. Forman discusses the characteristics of the new technological media and traces the implications of kinetic print for cognitive development. He also speculates about the future forms of computers for young children.

1

Moving the focus to middle childhood and adolescence, Dennis Wolf in Chapter Three describes research on the creation of text on the computer. Computers may be very useful as tools to enhance not only the writer's ability to create and edit text but also the researcher's ability to keep track of and make sense of the writing process. The findings of the research are discussed in terms of developmental differences in editing procedures and of the contributions of the interactive medium to the process.

My research on the role of the computer in the development of imagery skills and spatial thought is examined in Chapter Four. Presentation of important visual and spatial information (such as rotations, transformations, enlargements, and so forth) in an interactive format makes the computer a unique tool for experiences with imagery and for developing knowledge about space. I present results from a study in which children, adolescents, and young adults solved equivalent imagery problems in two different media, video and computer. The findings are discussed with respect to the nature of the symbolic content of computer interactions.

In Chapter Five, Roy Pea discusses the notion of integrated human-computer intelligent systems. Starting from the capabilities of computer expert or tutoring systems, Pea argues that such systems can be combined with human intellectual capacities to create a powerful means with which the child can solve complex problems. He speculates on the implications of computer applications and artificial intelligence for the study of development and learning.

In Chapter Six, Andrea diSessa explores the idea of the computer as an epistemological catalyst. Some students seem to have deep-seated expectations about what it is to know about certain subject matter. These expectations in turn directly affect what these students attend to, how they solve problems, and what they study and learn. Such epistemological knowledge may be crucial to developing better learners. The author presents two case studies of first-year university students that demonstrate remarkably different epistemologies with concomitant learning patterns and discusses opportunities and techniques for using computers to encourage learning about knowing.

Several themes run through the chapters in this volume. First, all the authors to some extent examine the notion that the computer enables the child to look at the world in a unique way. The second theme has to do with the creation of a new type of symbol system, which combines the qualities of movement and transformation with graphics and with text. The third theme involves the efficiency or ease with which the computer helps us to perform certain types of tasks and to solve particular problems. Finally and perhaps most important, all the authors speculate on the potential role of the computer in children's cognitive development. We have just begun to examine the many ways in which the computer may influence the child's construction of knowledge.

Elisa L. Klein
Editor

Reference

Papert, S. *Mindstorms: Children, Computers, and Powerful Ideas.* New York: Basic Books, 1980.

Elisa L. Klein is assistant professor of education at The Ohio State University. Her research interests concern cognitive development in children, including the development of mental imagery, and the role of computers in development and learning.

Children's use of computers to experiment and test ideas makes important contributions to their intellectual development, especially as they seek to construct theories about the nature of the physical world.

Computers in Early Education: The Child as Theory Builder

Christine Chaillé
Barbara Littman

The computer is a revolutionary tool that may have the potential to help children become more intelligent, effective individuals in a complex world. This chapter presents the thesis that children's use of computers to experiment and test ideas in ways not possible or feasible in other media may make important contributions to their intellectual development. The chapter begins with a discussion of the nature of intelligence from a constructivist perspective, focusing on how such intelligence can be fostered by engaging in theory-oriented problem solving. Following this is a brief presentation of ways in which computers are currently being used with adults and older children in a variety of domains to foster theory-oriented problem-solving abilities. In the next section, we consider how a theory-oriented problem-solving approach to computer use with older people may stimulate children's efforts to construct theories about the nature of the physical world. In the last section, we suggest that this approach could profitably be explored in a variety of learning domains, with some practical and theoretical implications.

E. L. Klein (Ed.). *Children and Computers.* New Directions for
Child Development, no. 28. San Francisco: Jossey-Bass, June 1985.

6

Intelligence and Theory-Oriented Problem Solving

Constructivist theory defines intelligence as the ability to acquire and adapt knowledge and skills in a wide range of contexts (Piaget, 1973, 1977). Applying knowledge in a wide range of contexts requires generalization from the situation in which knowledge was acquired to other more or less similar situations. In order to establish continuity across settings, it is necessary to abstract from learning situations the features and processes relevant for performing similar activities in different contexts and then to base predictions and inferences about what might happen in a new setting on those abstractions (Forman and Kuschner, 1984).

Only by having a theory or underlying unifying principle that serves the function of interpreting experience can one engage in the predictive and inferential thinking necessary to connect novel or contradictory experiences with familiar experiences (Karmiloff-Smith and Inhelder, 1974). Theory-oriented efforts to account for experience constitute a dynamic, cyclic process of formulating, testing, and modifying theories about the way the world works (Piaget, 1977).

Theory-oriented problem solving involves a focus on means: on relationships, processes, and principles. In contrast, success-oriented problem solving involves a focus on goals and end points (Karmiloff-Smith and Inhelder, 1974). The structural difference between success-oriented and theory-oriented problem solving can have significant cognitive consequences. An individual engaged in success-oriented problem solving, focusing only on a goal or end point, may succeed at a task without necessarily understanding the underlying reasons for success (Piaget, 1976, 1978). Thus, while the individual can be successful at a given task, he or she may be incapable of transferring an effective strategy to another context. When an individual engages in theory-oriented problem solving, the focus on underlying means and principles provides an awareness of why something occurs (Forman and Edwards, 1982; Karmiloff-Smith and Inhelder, 1974). It is this awareness of the why that allows the individual to hypothesize about other related problems (Piaget, 1976; Sinclair, 1978). It allows intelligent, effective behavior in a range of settings.

Research conducted in a variety of learning domains and across age groups suggests certain factors that contribute to the ability to generalize knowledge across contexts. There is evidence that opportunities for exploration (Kuhn, 1981), trial and error (Greenfield and Lave, 1982), and interaction with open-ended materials (Duckworth, 1973;

Pepler and Ross, 1981) foster the testing of multiple hypotheses and the consideration of numerous possible solutions to a given problem. One reason why these factors may facilitate generalization is that they stimulate the learner to focus on means rather than on ends, thereby fostering a theory orientation in problem solving. Problem-solving appears to be facilitated in a context in which the testing of both correct and incorrect theories is allowed and indeed encouraged.

Since understanding, not merely success, is the goal of theory-oriented problem solving, the holding of incorrect or incomplete theories can be an important source of the conflict needed to stimulate reformulation of hypotheses (Forman, 1981; Karmiloff-Smith and Inhelder, 1974). For example, Pepler and Ross (1981) found that children who acquired information in a convergent problem-solving context in which testing of multiple hypotheses was not possible did not modify or abandon ineffective strategies. In contrast, children who acquired similar information in a divergent problem-solving context tested many possible solutions, some of which were in fact wrong, but rapidly modified or abandoned the inappropriate solutions. Thus, contexts in which children have opportunities to make errors also encourage efforts to reconcile discrepancies between observed events and the predictions that the individual is making. These efforts in turn result in formulation of increasingly comprehensive theories to account for experience (Kuhn, 1981; Piaget, 1980). These increasingly comprehensive theories provide a basis for accounting for an even wider range of experiences, allowing more effective behavior across an increasing range of settings (Forman and Kuschner, 1984).

Glaser (1984) argues that the acquisition and application of knowledge in the context of hypothesis formation and testing just described stimulate the self-regulatory processes required for effective problem solving. Glaser suggests that acquisition of knowledge in a context that requires self-monitoring for effective problem solving improves problem representation and that the ability to generalize knowledge is in large part a function of the quality of one's representations.

A number of researchers have suggested that an awareness of critical features of events and processes is another important contributor to effective problem representations and hence to the ability to generalize (Copple and others, 1979; Forman and Kuschner, 1984). Awareness of critical features of events and processes provides the basis for reflecting on the underlying principles and mechanisms at work in a given situation. As noted earlier, such reflection allows one to understand why something occurs and then to generalize that understanding to a range of contexts. Thus, by contributing to the formation of effective problem representations that can be used in a range of contexts, awareness of critical features of events and processes is an important factor in generalization of knowledge across settings.

Computers and Theory-Oriented Problem Solving

Computers are increasingly being used to allow older children and adults to test ideas in unique ways. By providing such experiences, computers have the capacity to help people shift from a success orientation to a theory orientation in problem solving. Computers are currently being used to facilitate this shift in the areas of mathematics, literacy, art, and science. One good example in mathematics involves the use of the programming language LOGO, which makes both mathematical abstractions and the programming process concrete (Papert, 1980). In another area, word processing is being used to free people from the laborious revision and cleanup work needed in writing and thus to encourage them to focus on ideas and the playful use of language rather than on the mechanical aspects of written language (McWilliams, 1982; Paisley and Chen, 1982). Computer-aided design (CAD) provides a mechanism allowing architects, engineers, and artists to experiment rapidly with a variety of graphic and structural design elements in ways that are simply not possible with other representational media (Dameron, 1982; Leavitt, 1976).

In other domains, computer-generated images are being used in physical and biological science research to understand complex molecular structures. Before computer-generated images were available, a lack of precise knowledge about structure made further theoretical inquiry difficult or impossible. In physics, computer simulations of physics experiments are increasingly being used to give abstract and relatively inaccessible concepts concrete form (Champagne and others, 1980). One particularly interesting approach to making physics concrete for older children is seen in the work of diSessa (1982 and Chapter Six in this volume). In a computer-simulated gravity-free environment, adolescents develop an understanding of abstract laws of physics by experimenting with force and direction to guide a dyna-turtle.

In the field of early childhood education, however, applications of the computer as a tool allowing users to focus on the testing of ideas are relatively few. Because this approach may help children to become more effective, intelligent individuals, we feel that it should be one of the most actively pursued avenues of applications. In our own work, we have used an approach similar to diSessa's to examine how children's use of computer simulations and related objects can foster their theory-oriented problem-solving abilities in the domain of physics. While the development of children's theories about the nature of the physical world is of particular interest to us, we hope to see research consistent with our perspective that addresses other learning domains, such as oral and written language, graphic arts, and music.

Focusing on Physical Knowledge

A significant portion of young children's spontaneous motoric and intellectual activity is devoted to exploring the nature of the physical world. Constructivists refer to the child's acquisition and construction of knowledge about the physical world as *physical knowledge acquisition* (Kamii and DeVries, 1978; Piaget, 1970, 1976). The spontaneous activity of physical knowledge acquisition is actually a process of theory building directed toward the end of developing rudimentary unifying principles of physics (Piaget and Garcia, 1974). This theory building involves children's understanding of the behavior of objects and materials in terms of their attributes: Spheres roll, cubes do not, and cylinders—which simultaneously possess both curved and linear attributes—may or may not roll depending on the forces exerted. This brief description of object behaviors reveals the complexity of object attribute and behavior variables, which the child must coordinate as he or she formulates and tests even simple ideas about objects. Since such theory building requires the child to abstract empirical relationships from their interactions with objects as well as reflectively to abstract cognitive classes for comparing the effects produced on objects (Gallagher, 1978), it is a critical component of subsequent cognitive development (Kamii and DeVries, 1978; Piaget, 1977).

Children acquire or construct such knowledge first by hypothesizing about relationships between their own actions and the behavior of objects and materials, then by experimenting to test hypotheses, then by modifying their hypotheses as a result of the effects observed (Kamii and DeVries, 1978). However, many natural phenomena are difficult for children to understand despite experimentation with objects or materials. The information critical to understanding the processes involved in natural phenomena as well as the effects of the child's actions on those processes may be "invisible" or functionally inaccessible in traditional early childhood materials (Forman and Kuschner, 1984). For example, as children play with a pendulum, it frequently swings too rapidly for the trajectory to be observed. For the child, the trajectory arc is functionally inaccessible, since the child cannot see the results of his or her actions on it. Yet, information about how the child's actions on the object can produce a change in the trajectory arc may be critical in allowing the child to engage in theory-oriented experimentation, as he or she might do in the context of using swinging objects to knock over a target.

It is interesting to note here some innovative research that examined adult's and adolescent's understanding of principles of physics. McCloskey and his colleagues (McCloskey and others, 1980; McCloskey, 1983) found that, despite a lifetime of experience with moving objects, many adults hold naive theories about the behavior of moving objects. These researchers indicated that, when acquisition of knowledge about physical principles occurs in a context in which naive theories are not addressed, the resulting information will not necessarily result in modification of incorrect theories. Recently, McCloskey (1984) has suggested that naive theories of physics may even be the source of ineffective behavior. However, the work of diSessa (1982 and Chapter Six in this volume) provides encouraging insight into this issue. As mentioned earlier, diSessa examined how an individual's theories evolve during use of a computer-simulated gravity-free environment in which critical features of gravity principles are accessible. In this environment, an individual can engage in exploratory experimentation, formulating and testing multiple hypotheses about the phenomenon of gravity. Research results indicate that in this context the learner is able to resolve discrepancies between observed events and his or her predictions based on wrong or naive theories. In effect, diSessa's gravity-free environment provides the context we described earlier as stimulating theory-oriented problem solving. Later in this section, a similar approach to computer use with young children will be discussed that may stimulate them also to engage in theory-oriented problem solving.

If we accept, first, that the child's construction of physical knowledge may be problematic despite experimentation with materials and objects; second, that physical knowledge acquisition is critical for subsequent cognitive development; and, third, that opportunities for theory-oriented problem solving contribute to the intelligent adaptation of skills and knowledge across contexts, how can we foster children's theory-oriented efforts to understand the behavior of objects and materials?

Several early childhood educators with a Piagetian perspective (Kamii and DeVries, 1978; Forman and Kuschner, 1984; Forman and Hill, 1984) have formulated pedagogic guidelines for providing experiences that foster children's theory-oriented efforts to organize their experiences in the physical world. These guidelines function to provide children with opportunities for self-regulated exploratory activity in which critical aspects of processes and relationships are revealed in play materials.

Forman and his colleagues (Forman and Kuschner, 1984; Forman and Hill, 1984) describe the importance of structuring materials in such a way that children can test ideas about the behavior of objects and materials by making comparisons between dynamic transformations along a continuum rather than between static beginning and end points. Having access to dynamic transformations allows children to think about how something has happened, as opposed to thinking only about the end result. Going back to the example of swinging objects, Forman and Hill have designed a special piece of play equipment, a sand-dribbling pendulum, that records and reveals the spatial and temporal transformations that occur as an object swings between two points. While there are a number of interesting methods for stimulating children to think about the dynamic processes of phenomena, the sand-dribbling pendulum uses a technique of motion representation to provide children with a visual record of a movement process. This visual record reveals to children critical features of the pendulum's trajectory and allows them to reflect on the phenomena thus revealed in ways not otherwise possible. Through self-regulated exploratory play with materials structured to reveal process information, the child can engage in the theory-oriented activity of reflecting on means rather than ends. The child has the foundation for inferential and predictive thinking (Copple and others, 1979).

Kamii and DeVries (1978) identify four criteria for effective physical knowledge activities that, like the guidelines proposed by Forman and his colleagues, stimulate children to think about process and means, primarily by giving them access to and control over the variables in a given phenomenon: First, the child must be able to produce movement or change of objects by his or her own actions. Second, the child must be able to vary his or her actions to produce different effects. Third, the effects must be observable. Fourth, the effects must be immediate.

Returning to the pendulum example, we can incorporate these criteria into the design of play materials so that we can examine the ways in which their use provides opportunities for theory-oriented problem solving. To best illustrate the point, we will discuss the pendulum example (Figure 1). Children use the pendulum to try to hit plastic bowling pins. The first two columns of Table 1 relate each criterion for effective knowledge activities to each of the pendulum bowling variables.

Figure 1. Pendulum Bowling

In effect, Table 1 shows how materials can be structured to highlight processes, thus allowing children to use knowledge that is frequently inaccessible as a basis for theory building through meaningful experimentation.

Using Computers to Facilitate Physical Knowledge Acquisition

This section examines how the criteria for effective physical knowledge activities can be maximized by using computers to engage children in unique forms of experimentation. The computer's ability to represent, emphasize, and thus make accessible to children critical

Table 1. Pendulum Bowling: A Physical Knowledge Activity

Criterion	Object-Based Activity	Computer Simulation
Child produces movement or change.	Child can knock pins over. Child can move pins' placement. Pendulum swings when pulled back and released or is pushed by child. Pendulum knocks pin(s) over when accurately aligned.	Child can move pin(s) at any point during activity, even after pendulum release. Child can vary orientation during swing. Child can slow down swing speed to examine.
Child can vary actions.	Child can try a wide range of configurations. Child can vary the number of pins used. Child can release or push pendulum to exert different degrees of force from different spatial points. Child can swing or push pendulum a varying distance from pin(s) from any point in a 360° arc around pin(s).	
Reaction of objects is observable.	Pins either fall or remain standing. Pendulum swings in differing positions; position change is observable.	Pin or trajectory can be modified after release of pendulum to correct for errors. Ghost pin configuration can be left to compare with represented pendulum trajectories and fallen pins. Pendulum trajectory can easily be represented. Speed can be controlled. Imaginary trajectory can be called up prior to play.
Reaction of objects is immediate.	Pins fall or wobble immediately on contact with pendulum. Pendulum swings immediately when released or pushed. Pendulum swings immediately when released or pushed, immediately knocking pin(s) over or leaving them standing.	Pendulum trajectory representation can be observed. Comparison of ghost of pin and trajectory representation can be better observed.

features of phenomena and processes in an exploratory context will be explored.

The preceding section described ways in which play materials can be designed to provide children with access to critical information and relationships. Table 1 showed how pendulum bowling could be structured to highlight two things: the process of trajectory swing through a technique of motion representation, and phenomenon variables and the relationships between variables. We stated that access to and control over variables stimulates reflective thought about activity. We can hypothesize that some processes may be even more effectively highlighted by designing special computer simulations that children can use in conjunction with related object-based activities. For example, if the child could "see" an imaginary configuration of standing pins after they had been knocked over (Figure 2) and compare the initial pin configuration with the real pins when knocked over and the pendulum trajectory represented, he or she would have a wealth of information on which to draw for further theory building. The availability and salience of this information could stimulate the child to reflect on aspects of the problem not previously considered as well as provide information needed for continued theory building about the phenomenon in general. When the highlighted forms of information are incorporated into a

Figure 2. Simulated Pendulum Bowling with Process Highlighters

computer simulation, they are referred to as *process highlighters*. The rightmost column of Table 1 shows how process highlighters can be incorporated into a computer-simulated physical knowledge activity and how they supplement the means available to children for obtaining information.

Table 1 shows how computer-simulated process highlighters can maximize the criteria for effective physical knowledge activity development described earlier. If the computer provided children with access to such process highlighters as ghost representations of pin configurations, imaginary trajectories prior to release of the pendulum, and precise variations in the speed of the swinging pendulum, it could provide children with opportunities to experiment and test ideas in ways not possible in other media.

The kind of computer simulation just described lends itself well to the testing of multiple hypotheses through self-regulated exploratory activity. By configuring their own game, engaging in social interaction as they play, and posing novel problems with the materials, children can use a simulated bowling activity as they would an open-ended object-based bowling set. In addition, the computer simulation would make available process highlighters that the child could introduce into his or her own play at will. In theory, this could foster self-regulated awareness of critical features of the phenomena embodied in the activity.

Conclusion and Suggestions for Further Research

To summarize, in this chapter we have described a use of computers that could stimulate children's theory-oriented problem-solving abilities in one learning domain, physical knowledge acquisition. Three points about this approach have implications for other learning domains. First, we are not suggesting that computer experience is a substitute for experiences with objects or other media. On the contrary, it may be the combination of computer-based with object-based experiences that has the potential to foster intelligence. We need to consider which phenomena or learning domains may appropriately be explored with the aid of a computer. Some physical phenomena may not lend themselves to computer simulations.

Second, it is critical for children to have opportunities to use the computer in a social context of exploratory activity. Social interaction is an important contributor to cognitive development in general (Perret-Clermont, 1980) and to physical knowledge acquisition in particular (Kamii and DeVries, 1978; Verba and others, 1982).

Third, the approach that we suggest considers the computer as simply one more tool that children can use in an exploratory, open-ended manner. It is a tool that allows multiple strategies and the testing of dynamic theories and individual style differences to come into play during exploratory activity. If the computer is viewed as a tool similar in its flexibility to finger paint and unit blocks, it may have the potential to provide children with opportunities to engage in meaningful theory building.

Research into the contributions that computers can make into young children's theory-oriented problem-solving abilities is needed in a variety of learning domains. Such research is necessary to answer the important questions of how, when, and in fact whether microcomputers can appropriately be used to foster cognitive development in young children. By formulating research questions that look at the computer's ability to provide or extend experiences in ways not possible in other media, we can begin to answer these questions. Our own current research, which examines children's strategies in exploring computer simulations that include process highlighters, is one approach to these questions.

Looking at the contributions that microcomputers may make to children's theory-oriented efforts to understand the physical world has a number of theoretical and practical implications. First, if children's use of process highlighters does in fact permit them to abstract the critical features, events, and processes of phenomena and if it promotes reflective thought about these things, we may gain insight into the meta-cognitive processes of children's theory building. By giving children access to and control over process highlighters, we can observe more directly than we could in the past the factors that influence the genesis and use of problem-solving strategies. The resulting information could help us to expand children's strategy repertoires as well as provide them with direct insight into their own strategies.

Second, use of computer simulations by young children may provide information on which to base meaningful descriptions of the nature and role of action in cognitive development. Specifically, the computer may be particularly useful as a tool for studying the role of action in disabled children's cognitive development as well as for providing such children with a mechanism that enables them to manipulate the environment (Goldenberg, 1979).

Third, the use of process highlighters as a mechanism for understanding the process of physical knowledge construction in children may reveal underlying causes for the failure to achieve formal thinking ability seen in many adolescents and adults as well as causes for differences in girls' and boys' performance in mathematics and science (Kirk, 1975). Children's early actions on objects and the schemes they develop for sorting, comparing, and classifying objects are critical to subsequent cognitive development. If we can uncover and understand the differences and similarities between girls' and boys' theory-oriented problem-solving strategies, both with objects and with computers, we may be able to provide all children with experiences that will foster later interest and participation in mathematics and science (Block, 1983).

We would like to suggest one last, particularly important implication — an implication relevant to children's computer use in a range of learning domains: If computer use is practiced and studied along the lines described in this chapter, it could help to produce a generation of individuals who are not only computer literate but who are capable of intelligently organizing knowledge and skills so as to be effective in a wide range of contexts.

References

Block, J. H. "Differential Premises Arising from Differential Socialization of the Sexes: Some Conjectures." *Child Development,* 1983, *54,* 1335–1354.

Champagne, A. B., Klopfer, L. E., and Anderson, J. H. "Factors Influencing the Learning of Classical Mechanics." *American Journal of Physics,* 1980, *48,* 1074–1079.

Copple, C., Sigel, I., and Saunders, R. *Educating the Young Thinker.* New York: D. Van Nostrand, 1979.

Dameron, D. "Computer Sculpture." *The Computing Teacher,* January 1982, pp. 12–15.

diSessa, A. A. "Unlearning Aristotelian Physics: A Study of Knowledge-Based Learning." *Cognitive Science,* 1982, *6,* 37–75.

Duckworth, E. "The Having of Wonderful Ideas." In M. Schwebel and J. Raph (Eds.), *Piaget in the Classroom.* New York: Basic Books, 1973.

Forman, G. "The Power of Negative Thinking: Equilibration in the Preschool." In I. E. Sigel, D. M. Brodzinsky, and R. Golinkoff (Eds.), *New Directions in Piagetian Theory and Practice.* Hillsdale, N.J.: Erlbaum, 1981.

Forman, G., and Edwards, C. *The Use of Stopped-Action Video Replay to Heighten Theory Testing in Young Children Solving Balancing Tasks.* Final Report, NIE Grant G–81–0095. Washington, D.C.: National Institute of Education, 1982.

Forman, G., and Hill, D. F. *Constructive Play: Applying Piaget in the Preschool.* Reading, Mass.: Addison-Wesley, 1984.

Forman, G., and Kuschner, D. *The Child's Construction of Knowledge: Piaget for Teaching Children.* Washington, D.C.: NAEYC, 1984.

Gallagher, J. "Reflexive Abstraction and Education." In J. Gallagher and J. Easley (Eds.), *Knowledge and Development.* Vol. 2: *Piaget and Education.* New York: Plenum, 1978.

Glaser, R. "Education and Thinking: The Role of Knowledge." *American Psychologist,* 1984, *39,* 93–104.

Goldenberg, P. *Special Technology for Special Children.* Baltimore, Md.: University Park Press, 1979.

Greenfield, P. M., and Lave, J. "Cognitive Aspects of Informal Education." In D. A. Wagner and H. W. Stevenson (Eds.), *Cultural Perspectives on Child Development.* San Francisco: W. H. Freeman, 1982.

Kamii, C., and DeVries, R. *Physical Knowledge in Preschool Education.* Englewood Cliffs, N.J.: Prentice-Hall, 1978.

Karmiloff-Smith, A., and Inhelder, B. "If You Want to Get Ahead, Get a Theory." *Cognition,* 1974, *3* (195), 212.

Kirk, B. A. *Factors Affecting Young Women's Direction Toward Science, Technology, Mathematics.* Berkeley, Calif.: Management Technology Careers Projects, 1975.

Kuhn, D. "The Role of Self-Directed Activity in Cognitive Development." In I. E. Siegel, D. M. Brozinsky, and R. Golinkoff (Eds.), *New Directions in Piagetian Theory and Practice.* Hillsdale, N.J.: Erlbaum, 1981.

Leavitt, R. (Ed.). *Artist and Computer.* New York: Harmony Press, 1976.

McCloskey, M. "Intuitive Physics." *Scientific American,* April 1983, pp. 122–130.

McCloskey, M. "Cartoon Physics." *Psychology Today,* April 1984, pp. 52–58.

McCloskey, M., Caramazza, A., and Green, B. "Curvilinear Motion in the Absence of External Forces: Naive Beliefs About the Motion of Objects." *Science,* 1980, *210,* 1139–1141.

McWilliams, P. *The Word Processing Book.* New York: Prelude Press, 1982.

Paisley, W., and Chen, M. *Children and Electronic Text: Challenge and Opportunity of New Literacy.* Stanford, Calif.: Stanford University Institute for Communication Research, 1982.

Papert, S. *Mindstorms: Children, Computers, and Powerful Ideas.* New York: Basic Books, 1980.

Pepler, D. J., and Ross, M. S. "The Effects of Play on Convergent and Divergent Problem Solving." *Child Development,* 1981, *52,* 1201–1210.

Perret-Clermont, A. *Social Interaction and Cognitive Development in Children.* New York: Academic Press, 1980.

Piaget, J. *The Child's Concept of Movement and Speed.* New York: Basic Books, 1970.

Piaget, J. *To Understand Is to Invent: The Future of Education.* New York: Grossman, 1973.

Piaget, J. *The Grasp of Consciousness: Action and Concept in the Young Child.* Cambridge, Mass.: Harvard University Press, 1976.

Piaget, J. *The Equilibration of Cognitive Structures.* New York: Grossman, 1977.

Piaget, J. *Success and Understanding.* Cambridge, Mass.: Harvard University Press, 1978.

Piaget, J. *Experiments in Contradiction.* Chicago: University of Chicago Press, 1980.

Piaget, J., and Garcia, R. *Understanding Causality.* New York: Norton, 1974.

Sinclair, H. "Conceptualization and Awareness in Piaget's Theory and Its Relevance to the Child's Conception of Language." In A. Sinclair, R. S. Jarvella, and W. S. Levett (Eds.), *The Child's Conception of Language.* Berlin: Springer Verlag, 1978.

Verba, M., Stamback, M., and Sinclair, H. "Physical Knowledge and Social Interaction in Children from 18–24 Months of Age." In G. Forman (Ed.), *Action and Thought: From Sensorimotor Schemes to Symbolic Operations.* New York: Academic Press, 1982.

Christine Chaillé is assistant professor of education at the University of Oregon, where she does research on children's cognitive development and early education.

Barbara Littman, formerly a student at the University of Oregon, designs toys and materials for young children.

The young child can use computer graphics to invent and manipulate symbols in a variety of ways. The result is a new type of symbol, kinetic print.

The Value of Kinetic Print in Computer Graphics for Young Children

George Forman

This chapter explores the educational value of computer graphics for young children. These graphics include anything from animated cartoon characters to simulated pinball games. On the computer screen, these symbolic objects can move on their own, or they can be moved by the child. In contrast to computer graphics, ordinary printed symbols, such as a snapshot of a sports event, a printed sentence, or a musical score, are stationary. Film and television certainly use kinetic images, but they are not interactive, and thus they do not allow children to use kinetic images to represent their own ideas. Of the two, only film can be replayed. Videotape is interactive, and it can be replayed, but it presents only pictorial images. These constrasts bring us to the unique features of computer graphics: First, the symbols can be invented and constructed by the child. Second, the child can then move them directly on screen or give instructions to the computer to move them later.

E. L. Klein (Ed.). *Children and Computers.* New Directions for
Child Development, no. 28. San Francisco: Jossey-Bass, June 1985.

Third, the symbols can be anything from cartoon objects to lines, numbers, sounds, printed words, synthesized voice sounds, or three-dimensional objects, such as robots. Fourth, they can be rearranged and replayed again and again. The phrase *playable replayables* nicely captures both the interactive and the replayable features of computer graphics for young children. The phrase *kinetic print* nicely captures the points that can be made about symbols that move.

To what extent can children have more powerful thoughts through the use of symbols that move? This chapter begins with the proposition that symbolic development in the first seven years of life will be different for children who work with kinetic symbols on computers. The current literature locates the origins of symbolic development in natural language, drawing, and symbolic play with replica objects. Symbolic play with computer objects is sufficiently unique to merit a new program of research on symbolic development.

Symbolic Development

Symbolic development can be described in terms of several shifts. In the first year of life, the child can certainly solve problems, but at this age, actions are like tiny scripts (schemes) that play themselves out in the same sequence each time. The child can not pluck the middle out of an action scheme as an intact module and apply it elsewhere as a subroutine in the service of several different goals. At approximately one-and-one-half years of age, the child begins to separate means from ends and to think about pieces of the action flow as flexible units (Kessen and Nelson, 1978).

This shift, called *decontextualization,* is as important to symbolic development as it is to motor development (Greenfield and Smith, 1976). For example, the word *chair* may refer to the entire sequence of climbing in and sitting down on the chair. Or, the child might dial Mommy's office number correctly on a rotary phone but not on a push-button phone. Gradually, the child develops the skill to reflect on object states independent of the action flow, a shift that Mandler (1983) calls the transition from procedural to declarative representation. The procedural symbols represent knowledge of a specific sequence of acts, while declarative symbols represent knowledge that goes beyond a specific sequence. Imagine a child who can not only tell a visiting aunt how to get from his home to his school but who can also tell her how to get there via routes that he has never actually traveled.

Declarations on Procedures

As wonderful as the transition from rigid procedural knowledge to flexible declarative knowledge is, we may have been overly socialized to think in terms of declarations about what things are. Take the example of fist, a case often used by the late Alan Watts: Where is my fist when I open my hand? Words have a way of collapsing the implied action, and thus we forget that fist is an event rather than object.

The transition from procedural to declarative knowledge should not cause the dynamic to be replaced with the static. The effective thinker can integrate both types of knowledge into a single symbol system. The flow of experience is digitized into declarations that mark the boundaries of events, but the boundaries are understood as momentary points in time or as convenient perspectives only. For example, a rectangle is best understood as a convenient pause in the transformation of some other closed figure, such as a square, of which the rectangle is but the current boundary. Treating the rectangle not only as a shape but as an event makes it possible for the child to predict such things as area conservation or nonconservation after assorted transformations of the rectangle take place (Forman and Kuschner, 1984). By combining the point-fixing (static) quality of declaratives with the point-moving (dynamic) quality of procedures, children construct a symbol system that helps them to think flexibly about action patterns.

However, our conventional symbolic vehicles, such as print and discrete utterances, may have given us a bias toward treating events as objects (Gross, 1974). In point of fact, the invention of the differential in calculus was retarded by a bias against unbounded continua. Eventually, the calculus was systematized as the integration of the concept of limits with the concept of whole numbers. In calculus, limits are continuous functions that approach an end point, rather than the end point itself. Thus the concept of limits represented a major intellectual departure from early mathematics, characterized as it was by a strict adherence to the discrete categories of logic (Boyer, 1949). Could a new type of symbol system reduce our tendency to collapse the time within events?

Kinetic Print

Technology has now given us the means to construct symbol systems that use packets of action as an alphabet, a *kinetic print*. Kinetic print is more than a static notation of kinetic events, such as

22

Labanotation or a musical score. Kinetic print is movement used to make declarations about movement. Consider this example: A child is working on a ten-piece jigsaw puzzle. The formboard is actually a life-size image on a computer monitor, and the pieces are displayed around the border of the formboard image. The child used an electronic pen called a light pen to move any piece by touching it on the screen; the child presses a button again to pick the piece up, and rotates the piece by turning the light pen itself.

So far, we have nothing more than the equivalent of an ordinary jigsaw puzzle. But the computer reveals its unique contribution in what the child can do next. At any point in the puzzle-solving process, the child can see a replay of the pieces as moved (Figure 1), a replay of the action paths alone (Figure 2), or a piece-by-space notation of past moves in an alphanumeric code similar to that used in chess play (Figure 3). These representations are compiled automatically by the computer and retrieved at will by the child. Each representation not only captures the actual trial and error of past moves but also offers its own type of advantage.

The replay of pieces as moved (Figure 1) gives the child a chance to observe his or her attempts without having to think about making the action. The child is free to think ahead to the reasons behind an action; he or she is not distracted by making a controlled execution.

The replay of action paths (Figure 2) is more abstract than the watching of jigsaw pieces being moved on the screen. The child sees a

Figure 1. The Computer Replays the Movements of Puzzle Pieces

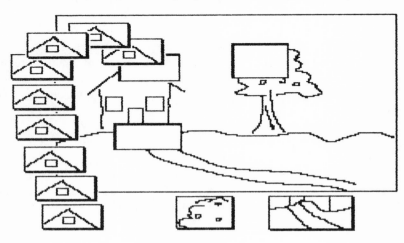

Figure 2. The Computer Replays the Action Paths of Puzzle Pieces

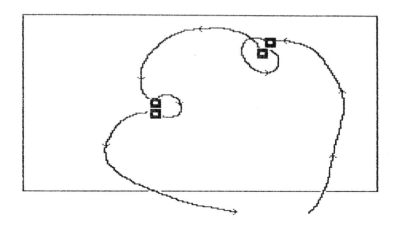

trail line that grows and indicates where the pieces make contact with the formboard, where they are rotated, where they are shifted to new spaces, and where they are removed from the formboard. To reduce clutter, the computer displays a trail line only if a particular piece is moved. The display resets to a blank screen when the child shifts to a new piece. The trail lines for different pieces have different colors, but the identity of the piece itself is not preserved in this representation. By

Figure 3. The Computer Replays a Piece-by-Space Notation of Puzzle Piece Moves

```
PIECE   -   SPACE(S)

X - 6 ' 5 ' 4 '

Q - 3 '

R - 3 '

W - 3 '

X - 5 , 5 , 4 , 4 '

ETC.
```

eliminating the identity of the piece, the computer leads the child to think about action routines per se, such as a bias toward fitting pieces or toward filling spaces (Forman and others, 1971).

The alphanumeric code gives a higher compressed notation of the past moves through the jigsaw space. For example, putting piece X in space 6 and then removing it without rotation can be coded X–6'. The subsequent moves X–5' and X–4' show that the child is repeatedly trying to place the same piece in different spaces. The code atemporal-izes the action flow (Forman, 1982) and thereby gives it sufficient invariance to help the child identify general patterns. The problem, of course, is that the code type of symbol system is too abstract for young children.

All three symbol systems represent events, but they differ in the nature of the relation between the symbol and the event itself. The computer replay of the jigsaw piece is primarily an analog to the event that it represents. An analog is a symbol that preserves many of the spatial and temporal aspects of the event that it represents. An analog symbol, such as a film, can best be contrasted with the digital symbol. The digital symbol, such as a printed sentence, is a string of discrete bits that share no spatial or temporal similarity with the event represented. The alphanumeric code is exclusively digital. The trail lines are both digital, in that they are discrete, well-bounded bits (from pick up to release), and analog, in that they embody spatial and temporal properties of the represented event. The trail lines are kinetic print — part analog, part digital. It is the premise of this chapter that kinetic print creates a mind-set more likely to combine the advantages of both procedural and declarative knowledge.

Animated Cartoons

The computer program just described has not to my knowledge been designed as yet. It was presented only to provide motive and definition. There are current products that either embody this notion of kinetic print or have potential in that direction. Some of these products are being used at the University of Massachusetts Child Development Center. For seven years, the program for three- to five-year-olds has been devoted to an implementation of curriculum based on Piaget's theory of development (Forman and Kuschner, 1984; Forman and Hill, 1984). We are continuing this tradition in our observations on how children interact with electronic media (Forman and others, 1982; Forman, 1984).

Since spring 1984, we have been watching children play with a

Coleco Industries product called Smurf Paint and Play Workshop. Two children sit in front of a color television set in order to give joystick commands to Smurf characters. The children can make the characters walk in any direction on the screen and even twirl the character by making a rotatory action with the joystick. The child can make the character jump, fall, or move into a new scene; each act is signaled by its own special sound effect. The child can also change the identity of the character by pressing a button, even as the character is moving. The scenes can be changed completely by pressing a button, or a given scene can be modified by adding preformed objects from a menu or by painting objects with an electronic paint brush controlled by the joystick. The child can also animate preformed and painted objects by placing these objects in different positions on four blank screens, recording any desired sequence of the four screens, then replaying the screens in the sequence in which they were recorded. The child has four basic choices: He or she can select ready-made objects or construct them, and he or she can select ready-made actions or construct them. The ready-made objects and actions are selected with the push buttons, and the constructions are executed with the joystick. All the child's choices can be recorded and replayed at will.

Elsewhere, I detail what children learn from this electronic symbolic play (Forman, 1984); here I will focus on the contrast between three different means of representation: the on-line movement of characters with the joystick, the replay of the character movements, and symbolic play with a three-dimensional Smurf doll house that we built to replicate the scenes and objects in the Paint and Play Workshop.

Our initial observations of children three to five years old indicate that they reflect more on process in the electronic medium and more on content in the three-dimensional medium. Comments in the doll house were primarily about who was who and why the doll was doing something; to put it more formally, the comments focused on character identity and personal motive. In contrast, in Paint and Play, children generally announced where they were going and what their character was about to do; they made declarations about direction and motion.

Two constraints could account for the salience of place and action in the electronic medium. First, the performatory demands are novel and require attention in order to get from here to there. This performatory demand then finds its way into the content of symbolic play (Olson, 1970). For another, the action on the screen is dislocated from the hand actions that produce screen effects, thereby infusing the screen characters with an illusion of self-agency. Children are intrigued with movement that can be directed from a distance. As one child said, "I can make my Smurf go anywhere, even outside."

Record and Replay

The most exciting feature of this product is the record and replay function. The children can make their Smurf jump a river, climb a tree, go inside a house, take a bath, and so on, all the while knowing that they are recording this action sequence. An interesting attitude change occurs once children understand that recording means they can see a replay. They become more reflective on what they are doing and more inventive in the actions created. After all, why record something dull? Several four-and-a-half-year-olds created identifiable episodes within the stream of play just so they could look for that episode in replay. They then were able to tell a playmate or teacher watching the replay just when that episode was about to occur. The three- and early four-year-olds preferred not to give up control of the Smurf to the replay mode. Their delight came more in on-line construction than in instant replay. They knew that the replay would act out their previous choices, but they just did not find it that interesting.

Our observations of the record and replay function suggest that replay is powerful only if the child thinks about the future when constructing the present action on line. This type of double perspective is difficult for three- and early four-year-olds, but it is commonplace in the four- and five-year-olds. The four- and five-year-olds create favorite little action motifs that they replay again and again. These replayable kinetic bits engender a declarative attitude toward the dramatic events (for example, goal, motive, conflict, and resolution). Thus, the kinetic motif serves the purpose of preserving the temporal flow of procedural knowledge while abstracting the uniform meaning of declarative knowledge. While action motifs do occur with the replica toys, they could never assume the declarative status of action that is replayed on a computer.

Touch Pad Graphics

We have been observing children use a graphics peripheral produced by Koala Technologies called the Koala Pad. The Koala Pad allows the child to draw images on the monitor by rubbing a blunt stylus on a four-inch-square touch tablet. The child can select brush width, color, and a number of interesting geometric functions. Everything is done by positioning a point of light on the screen. The point of light is positioned by moving the stylus on the touch tablet; a decision is executed by pressing a button.

Of course, there is nothing kinetic about a finished pattern on the monitor, but the drawing process offers some interesting contrasts with crayon and pencil. Take the geometric function called Boxes. When this function is selected, the child can draw rectangles of any size by stretching an electronic rubber band. The child presses the button to anchor the left corner of the rectangle and then stretches the rectangle to any size or proportion desired. Using a stretching procedure to draw rectangles, rather than drawing four straight lines, could well give children a different mind-set about geometric figures. This view fits well with earlier discussions of the importance of continuous transformations (Forman, 1974, 1981). When one thinks about continuous transformations, such as what happens to the area of a rectangle when it is flattened slightly, one is more likely to understand that its area is not conserved. Adults have a tendency to conclude that area is conserved (Forman and Kuschner, 1984), but today's adults have not been raised with kinetic print all around them.

Kinetic images are also part of a Koala Pad function called Area Fill. The child can draw any figure on the screen using loopbacks and other ways of making closed areas. Then, by placing the cursor light inside the pattern, the child can cause the computer to color in all the contiguous vacant space. Our four- and five-year-olds were challenged as they tried to predict whether pressing the fill button would color only a small portion of the drawing or cause the color to bleed into the background as well. Through the power of colors that move, children learn that topological features, such as closure, are consequences of actions, not static shapes.

Light Pens

We have done some preliminary observations of children using the Gibson Light Pen distributed by Koala Technologies. The light pen allows the child to draw figures by touching the pen directly to the screen. The child can fill in areas; duplicate, move, or stretch the objects that he or she draws; and do mirror drawing in four-part harmony (the computer mirrors anything drawn in both right-left and up-down symmetry). Children can even type words, then pick them up and move them around on the screen like felt pieces on a felt board. The software also includes a cartoon animation kit for twenty-frame sequences.

At first, children are amazed at making marks directly on the computer screen. The mirror drawings seem to be the most fascinating. Even a scribble has an elegant symmetry, much like the random chips of glass in a kaleidoscope. The children have an equal fascination with making marks by erasing black; that is, they etch marks by subtracting color rather than by adding color. My own experience shows how working with the light pen can change how one thinks about a line drawing. Once one knows that anything drawn can be duplicated, moved, or stretched, the line drawing comes alive with potential. When drawing objects, I look for modules that can be drawn only once from scratch and then closed. For example, I draw one wheel, then clone three more and move them to new locations. To draw new perspectives, one can clone the original, then edit it slightly. Any objects to be redrawn can be quickly roughed out in a sketch. Then I can think about how to clone, stretch, and move the parts around until the drawing looks right. The greatest value of this tool exists when I draw three or four pictures of objects changing across time. Some objects are not moved between frames, and some objects are moved or deleted without much redrawing required.

The point of this example goes beyond the technology, as amazing as it may be. The point is in what the tool teaches. I read book illustrations differently now; I see that the chaise lounge is a stretched out chair and that I could reproduce that grassy texture by cloning a lot of W's. The medium, if used often enough, causes the user to internalize its inherent functions (Salomon, 1979). The kinetic possibilities of the medium produce a kinetic attitude toward static drawings. Drawings take on greater unity, since more of their parts are seen as transformations or duplications of other parts. This is no trivial pastime. The search for patterns is the primary purpose of the naturalist.

One other point can be made about drawing objects that change across time. With the light pen animator, one can run up to twenty drawings through a sequenced playback to see how the movement looks. If the user makes the drawings too different from one another, the movement looks too jerky, too similar, and too stationary. The light pen animator requires the user to digitize a continuous movement. While digitizing is too difficult for young children to do with the light pen, this process can be explored in a simplified fashion. At the University of Massachusetts preschool, we allowed children to roll spools down a ramp with speed bumps. The children could change the spacing of the speed bumps, notice the change in rhythm, and explore variations. The speed bumps converted a continuous action into discrete points. If the bumps were too close together, there was no rhythm at all. If they were too far apart, the long smooth intervals were prominent. Children soon discovered the spacing they needed in order to create an interesting clickety-clack. These preschoolers were exploring the world of intuitive calculus, at least at the practical level of digitizing an action into preferred units. Given the success of spools on speed bumps in the classroom, a light pen version might work as well. Moreover, the light pen has all the advantages of playback that I mentioned earlier. Of course, we would have to design new supporting software for young children to minimize the need for keyboard commands. The light pen in combination with activities like the rolling of spools can give children new ways of thinking about the digital within the analogical.

Putting the Classroom into the Computer

If teachers find it obtrusive to put the computer in the classroom, there are a host of ways to put the classroom into the computer. Special sensors that respond to light, sound, and pressure make it possible for children to gain a new understanding of their own habitat. Some of these devices have supporting software that are excellent examples of kinetic print, such as the AtariLab Temperature Module developed by Atari in collaboration with Dickenson College.

In AtariLab, a thermometer is connected to the computer display. Changes in temperature are displayed as a thermometer with the mercury at a certain height. The thermometer on the screen clones a duplicate every few seconds. If the temperature has decreased, the mercury level in the clone is lower. After several minutes, the computer converts the many thermometers into a conventional line graph that plots temperature against time.

These kinetic symbols — the thermometers moving from left to right — give more information than a static graph. The addition of real time — the pauses between clonings — helps the child to understand what the horizontal axis represents. There is some evidence that these kinetic images also help children to sense the paradox in plateaus (Tinker, 1983). While watching an image move horizontally for a time before continuing its descent, children begin to wonder what stopped the cooling during the plateau. Printed graphs pale in comparison with the computer's kinetic print. Furthermore, the child can vary the scale of graphs and instantly replay the same event on different graphs. The ease with which the computer allows the child to explore trains the child to distinguish physical facts from display artifacts, changes in events from changes in symbols.

Robots: Displays in Three Dimensions

There are few displays more captivating than a small robot being put through its paces. We have recently begun observing young children play with Robotix, a robot construction kit manufactured by Milton Bradley. The kit comes with four high-torque motors that can be configured in dozens of different moving machines — Star Wars walkers, hoists, robot arms — by snapping plastic limbs together. The motors are individually tethered by flexible wires to a console of rocker switches that activate each motor either forward or backward.

The educational value of these motorized toys is immense. Children can construct machines that must obey the laws of leverage, torque, and mass. Children also learn how to break actions down into on-line commands when manipulating, for example, small objects with a robot arm. These robots will yield other possibilities when they are connected to a microcomputer, which is not difficult to do. Unlike the LOGO robot turtle (Papert, 1980), Robotix can be configured at will by the child and move through all three planes of space.

For the purposes of this chapter, the question of interest is, What sort of code should young children use to talk to the computerized robot? I propose that this code should not be the alphanumeric code standard for LOGO programming. It makes more sense to let the child talk to the computer by moving a set of levers, or better yet, by moving the robot itself. The child could move the passive limbs in sequence. The computer then stores this sequence and activates the robot when the child presses the execute button. The young child can use all his or her knowledge of body movements to command the robot.

The true educational value of this arrangement comes from something the computer does in addition to making the robot move: The computer also displays on its screen kinetic symbols that represent action packets, such as a full turn of an arm or an opening of the fingers. Once the computer generates these little moving images that correspond to how the child manipulated the passive limbs, the child has the opportunity to edit a robot command by adding or rearranging the symbols on the screen, perhaps with a light pen. Thus, the child has two ways of creating intelligent action: by the analogical input from the passive robot, and by the rearrangement of the kinetic alphabet generated by the computer. Since the child created the referents for this alphabet in the first place, we can say that it is perfectly phonetic.

Children who can travel back and forth between analog and digital instructions to the robot should learn more than how to make the robot work. They should learn something about how their language works. For example, the symbols generated by moving the levers (and consequently the robot) cannot be edited with the light pen any way at all. Putting the symbol for opening the fingers immediately after the symbol for closing the fingers makes no sense pragmatically, but this sequence can be written in the code. Such a sequence of close and open actions is analogous to a double negative in English sentences. The symbol system has a syntax that must be learned, while the robot, as a physical system, has constraints known intuitively by the child. Traveling back and forth between the two systems helps the child to learn more about each. Experience gives meaning to language, and language gives understanding to experience. Furthermore, the kinetic aspect of these symbols, their rate of movement, timing, effort, and duration, should raise the child's awareness of the cinematic aspects of action. The cinematic aspects are the changes that, unlike direction and shape of action, cannot be represented very well in a static drawing. These aspects, which are important inflections in the linguistic sense, have been virtually ignored in current theory on symbolic development, except for work by Pierre Mounoud (Mounoud and Hauert, 1982).

Simulations

It is important for children to manipulate computer symbols that they understand. The Bill Budge Pinball Construction Kit by Electronic Arts is a good example of computer graphics that simulate real-world events. Children can construct their own playing surface in which a pinball can bounce and be kicked by flippers. If the space through which the pinball falls has deadspots, the child can reshape the borders and add bumpers to improve the game play. The child can even tamper with Newtonian parameters, such as gravity, elasticity, kick, and speed. This microworld becomes an experimental lab in which children can isolate variables, thereby determining their independent and combined effects.

We have observed early elementary grade children engrossed in this microworld, continuously editing the playing surface on the screen and experimenting with the laws of motion. If a wall has an inverse angle, the ball will be trapped, and the wall must be reshaped. If the gravity meter is set too high, the plunger spring will not have enough kick to get the ball out of the starting shoot. The child will either reduce the gravity or increase the kick. The fact that the child can make measured changes in the laws of nature creates a higher level of abstraction than ordinary play with real objects. Thus, the game encourages the children to think at multiple levels of abstraction, the visible event and the measurement of the visible event, which in turn leads the children to anticipate visible effects not yet seen.

The kinetic effects are highly repeatable around any given bumper or rail. The child can build a vocabulary of action motifs that can be arranged in a variety of combinations. And, like the symbolic code that instructs the robot, the play space constructed by the child "instructs" the pinball. The action motifs invented by the child are digital in that they can be defined and repeated and analog in their spatial and temporal similarity to the real objects that they represent.

Another example of computer simulations is still an idea, not an existing product. The world in this case is a microworld of blocks that can be moved around with a light pen. The child positions the light pen, presses a button to pick up the chosen block, moves it to a spot (in order, for example, to construct an arch), then presses the same button to release the block. The computer then simulates support or falling, whatever would happen if the computer symbols were real blocks. Figures 4 and 5 depict two frames in a game in which children are invited to build a roof to shelter a little person from the rain.

The advantage of computer simulations of block play come from three things: the mixture of icons, text, and directional arrows; the addition of dramatic tension to help the child sense the task objective; and the fact that at any point in play the child can repeatedly replay the last set of moves in order to reflect on his or her problem-solving strategies. In reference to the last objective, recent research has shown that confronting the child with a video replay of his or her block-balancing attempts encourages the child to take a more detached and strategic approach to the problems at hand (Forman and others, 1982). The

Figure 4. The Child Is Invited to Construct a Roof with Computer Block Icons

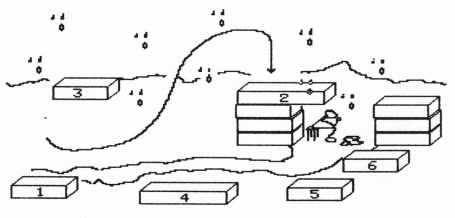

MAKE ME A ROOF WITH THE BLOCKS!

Figure 5. When the Child Releases Block Icons That Are Not Supported, The Blocks Fall

OOPS!   BETTER TRY AGAIN!

repeatable replay helps the child to convert procedural into declarative knowledge. Herein lies the power of the microcomputer for these open-ended problems.

Playable Replayables

To summarize the special advantages of computer graphics, I have coined the term *playable replayables.* Only through computer intelligence and speed can the child be presented with a representation of his or her own past trials and errors. The computer can instantly record the child's performance, translate the trials and errors into compact symbols (for example, the trail lines, moving blocks, and so forth) that can not only be observed but also edited, like words on a felt board. This proposed process is like building something with your hands, seeing the action typed as symbols, then moving the symbols around to see what construction the hand actions produce on the screen. The code flows from the manipulative performance, and then the code becomes an object with which to play. Of course, for young children (and I secretly hold the same view for adults), the code that flows from the manipulative performance should be represented by symbols that lie somewhere between pictures and words, dynamic symbols that are part digital and part analog. The most complete turn of phrase is this: Let children play with kinetic print replays of their own performance.

34

References

Boyer, C. B. *The History of the Calculus and Its Conceptual Development.* New York: Dover, 1949.

Forman, G. E. "Change Makes the Difference: Methods of Early Education Implicit in Piaget's Concept of Transformation." *Meforum,* University of Massachusetts, School of Education, Fall, 1974.

Forman, G. E. "The Power of Negative Thinking: Equilibration in the Preschool." In I. E. Sigel, D. M. Brodzinsky, and R. Golinkoff (Eds.), *New Directions in Piagetian Theory and Practice.* Hillsdale, N.J.: Erlbaum, 1981.

Forman, G. E. "A Search for the Origins of Equivalence Concepts Through a Microanalysis of Block Play." In G. Forman (Ed.), *Action and Thought: From Sensorimotor Schemes to Symbolic Operations.* New York: Academic Press, 1982.

Forman, G. E. "The Value of Computer Graphics for Young Children." Paper presented at the 3rd International Conference on Thinking, Cambridge, Mass., August 1984.

Forman, G. E., Fosnot, C., Edwards, C., and Goldhaber, J. *The Use of Stopped-Action Video Replay to Heighten Theory Testing in Young Children Solving Balancing Tasks.* Final Report, NIE Grant G-81-0095. Washington, D.C.: National Institute of Education, 1982.

Forman, G. E., and Hill, D. F. *Constructive Play: Applying Piaget in the Preschool.* Reading, Mass.: Addison–Wesley, 1984.

Forman, G. E., and Kuschner, D. S. *The Child's Construction of Knowledge: Piaget for Teaching Children.* Washington, D.C.: National Association for the Education of Young Children, 1984.

Forman, G. E., Laughlin, F., and Sweeney, M. "The Development of Jigsaw Puzzle Solving in Preschool Children: An Information-Processing Approach." *DARCEE Papers and Reports,* 1971, *5* (8), (entire issue).

Greenfield, P. M., and Smith, J. H. *The Structure of Communication in Early Language Development.* New York: Academic Press, 1976.

Gross, L. "Modes of Communication and the Acquisition of Symbolic Competence." In D. R. Olson (Ed.), *Media and Symbols: The Forms of Expression, Communication, and Education.* Chicago: University of Chicago Press, 1974.

Kessen, W., and Nelson, K. "What the Child Brings to Language." In B. Z. Presseisen, D. Goldstein, and M. H. Appel (Eds.), *Topics in Cognitive Development.* Vol 2: *Language and Operational Thought.* New York: Plenum, 1978.

Mandler, J. M. "Representation." In J. H. Flavell and E. M. Markman (Eds.), *Handbook of Child Psychology.* Vol. 3: *Cognitive Development.* New York: Wiley, 1983.

Mounoud, P., and Hauert, C. "Development of Sensorimotor Organization in Young Children: Grasping and Lifting Objects." In G. E. Forman (Ed.), *Action and Thought, From Sensorimotor Schemes to Symbolic Operation.* New York: Academic Press, 1982.

Olson, D. *Cognitive Development: The Child's Acquisition of Diagonality.* New York: Academic Press, 1970.

Papert, S. *Mindstorms: Children, Computers, and Powerful Ideas.* New York: Basic Books, 1982.

Salomon, G. *Interaction of Media, Cognition, and Learning: An Exploration of How Symbolic Forms Cultivate Mental Skills and Affect Knowledge Acquisition.* San Francisco: Jossey-Bass, 1979.

Tinker, R. Personal communication. August 1983.

Tymony, C. "Computer Control of a Video Recorder." *Byte,* July 1984, pp. 179–183.

George Forman is professor of early childhood education at the University of Massachusetts, Amherst. His research interests include the application of Piagetian theory to early education and the transition from sensorimotor intelligence to early symbolization.

Word processing may generate more than letter-perfect copy. When students use the editing capacities of microcomputers to the fullest, their efforts at reordering and deleting may provide insight into developmental differences in the writer's ability to create coherent texts.

Flexible Texts: Computer Editing in the Study of Writing

Dennis P. Wolf

The notion that computers may shed light on human competence is not new. Since computers first appeared, they have been used to promulgate and test models of human perception and information processing (Marr, 1984; Schank and Abelson, 1977). Much of the excitement about computers in developmental studies has come from the belief that computers will promote dramatic new concepts of learning and development. Thus, a number of writers have argued that children's performance on computers will force psychologists and educators to redraft long-accepted accounts of the limited nature of children's thinking processes (Greenfield, 1984; Papert, 1980). Other writers have argued that the computer screen will introduce individuals to a set of novel disciplines and problems, such as programming and the creation of kinetic displays, that will evoke previously unused capacities (Forman in Chapter Two of this volume).

However, it seems at least as likely that the power of computers to illuminate human thinking may lie in something like the opposite direction. That is, computers may also give researchers a second

E. L. Klein (Ed.). *Children and Computers.* New Directions for
Child Development, no. 28. San Francisco: Jossey-Bass, June 1985.

chance to examine old, difficult, or elusive issues in development and cognition. In this sense, computers may be to psychologists what new cultures are to anthropologists. In New Guinea or Sri Lanka, what seems ordinary or necessary can be apprehended anew. Thus, developmental or cognitive psychologists may be indentured to views of familiar processes, such as planning, problem solving, or writing, that could change in important ways if they were placed in the novel context of electronic memories, rotating two-dimensional images, or kinetic texts (Salomon, in press; Turkle, 1984).

Several examples spring to mind. First, researchers working on computer learning have had to reexamine questions about the focal or generalizable nature of human thinking skills by asking whether an ability, such as computer programming, is an isolated skill or a facet of some broader planning ability. Second, as we observe users working with microcomputers, received notions about the significance of certain ingredient skills within larger performances may shift considerably. Thus, the advent of calculators may cause the definition of early mathematical thinking to move away from arithmetic calculation and be redefined in terms of broader problem-generation and problem-solution skills. Similarly, certain characteristics of word processing, such as easy, rapid input and "cut-and-paste" options, may release writers from drudgery and in so doing reveal dimensions of the writing processes that were almost invisible in the past.

This chapter addresses the question of what we can find out about the development of writing skills from observing young writers at work on microprocessors. In particular, this chapter focuses on what we can learn about writing from studying writers as they make the kinds of large-scale revisions made possible by word processing software: reorderings, deletions, and insertions. Such revisions often rupture the original continuity of a piece of writing. Thus, by observing how writers of different ages ignore or address such ruptures, it is possible to map developmental changes in children's understanding of their writing as a continuous text.

Writing as Text Generation

Producing long pieces of writing—we can call them texts—is quite a demanding enterprise, because it requires the writer to generate and sustain different types of cross-sentence connections. At one level, a manuscript hangs together to the extent that the writer adheres more or less closely to a well-known format, such as the script for a familiar structure of a genre, such as folk or fairy tale (Mandler and Johnson, 1977; Rumelhart, 1975). In this case, coherence comes from including the expected elements in the canonical order.

Skilled writers also create a tightly knit fabric of syntactic and semantic ties across individual sentences. These ties include such links as those created by the use of indefinite, then definite articles (*a* boy. . . *the* boy. . . *that* boy); the use of pronominal forms to refer back to earlier nouns (the doctor. . . *he*. . .); and the recall of earlier events or settings (*there* she was, safely *at home again*) (Halliday and Hasan, 1976; van Dijk, 1972). Further, a writer may bind individual clauses or sentences together by supplying causal, logical, or psychological links between successive statements (Gardner, 1980; Slackman, 1984).

Finally, the very way in which an experienced writer selects words, phrasings, or details yields a text that promotes the sense of a particular scene, theme, or point of view. Thus, in writing about a meal, the occurrence of such words as *napkin, soup spoon, appetizer,* or *dessert* helps to glue the text together (Halliday and Hasan, 1976; Mandler, 1984). Alternatively, writers can select words so that they consistently suggest a continuous style or genre throughout a text. Thus, a science fiction writer may write *jagged asteriods floated aimlessly amidst vapors,* while a science reporter might write *star-like bodies have been observed to move in clouds of suspended particles* (Kress, 1982).

Microcomputers and the Study of Writing

When writers write smoothly, their performances are too seamless to provide much insight into the process of creating coherent texts. But luckily, few first drafts are flawless, and writers have to spend time revising their original raw materials. Literary critics and cognitive psychologists alike have pointed out that, when writers mend trouble spots, we get a critical view into otherwise sealed thinking processes (Jarrell, 1971; Nold, 1981; Perkins, 1981). Microcomputers may prove extremely useful in the study of writing precisely because of their power to reveal such editing behaviors (Daiute, 1984; Papert, 1980). Because electronic text is endlessly fixable, writing at a microcomputer can occur in a climate of risk taking. Since nothing a writer does is irreversible, it is safe to try a new word or to attempt a rephrasing. Moreover, microcomputer software makes text not only fixable but flexible. Unlike static text, in which large-scale editing is clumsy, electronic text can be reshuffled, expanded, or contracted with relative ease. Such options as scrolling and searching make it possible for writers to move rapidly from place to place in order to correct or shift their treatment of a particular topic. Thus, microcomputers make it possible for fairly young writers to attempt radical forms of editing on their own works in progress. In this way, microcomputers create the opportunity to analyze a very revealing level of editing behaviors even in relatively young writers.

The fixable and flexible qualities of computer writing create a kind of natural laboratory particularly suited to the examination of text-making skills. When writers revise, their efforts at reshuffling, deleting, and expanding text disrupt the connections that originally bound their texts together. Consider what happens when an eleven-year-old takes the suggestion to reverse the order of the first two paragraphs of a story. He uses the computer to reorder the first and second paragraphs of his text but fails to recognize most of the ambiguities and discontinuities that result.

Former Paragraph 2

Sylvester
~~He~~ sat at his desk shapening the chalk so it would squeak. Along came Marlo. Sylvester was still angry about those baseball facts. "Hmmm, time to pay the little runt back."

Former Paragraph 1

Sylvester Hufflanger was a mean crude and nasty fellow who hated kids badly. Unfortunately, he was also a sixth grade teacher. He spent a lot of time dreaming up terrible homework assignments, reasons for keeping kids after school and wicked comments to put on report cards. He especially hated Marlo who was a puny little kid who knew more baseball statistics than rules about long division.

In comparison, a skilled fourteen-year-old writer revises after she shuffles two paragraphs. She attempts to reestablish the connected or coherent quality of her text in a variety of ways.

Former Paragraph 2

Shira Limnock was younger,
When₍ ~~she~~ was small she had had a mother and a twin sister.
           especially   *parent*
Her mother had not₍ ~~particularly~~ wanted to be a₍ ~~mother~~. She was distressed to find herself the mother of two children. She didn't hate babies but she found caring for them tiresome — they couldn't talk yet, or even smile. . . . So she had arranged for herself to disappear and for the twins to be placed in a Children's Home.

Former Paragraph 1

Ever since then

∧All through her life Shira (who was outwardly practically perfect) had been haunted by the vague and rather disconcerting feeling that some part of her was missing...

In traditional writing media, it is rare for writers to attempt the kinds of revisions that demand this kind of repair work. Consequently, until the advent of computer writing, it was difficult to spot, never mind to analyze, the kinds of differences in young writers' text-making abilities that these two examples highlight.

The Design of the Study

During our study of text-making processes in computer writing, we observed two groups of young writers in both spontaneous writing and structured editing tasks. Four children aged eleven and twelve and four children aged between thirteen and fifteen were studied over a two-month period. At both of these ages, many children can write with sufficient fluency to generate long (100- to 300-word) texts in a single writing session. Yet there is evidence that preadolescents lack the systematic approach to problem solving that may make adolescents particularly well suited to the pursuit of consistent plans throughout a text (Inhelder and Piaget, 1958). The children were from middle-class backgrounds, and they had been selected by their classroom teachers as fluent writers for their age. In addition, they all had had enough computer writing experience so that they could both type and execute deletions, insertions, searches, and paragraph reversals with a minimum of adult help.

The students were observed writing at computers on three occasions at four-week intervals. During each collection period, children participated in three individual writing sessions, each lasting between thirty and forty-five minutes. The first session was designed to expose children's readily available text-making abilities, but young writers did little significant revising on their own. Consequently, the second and third sessions were designed to obtain a more detailed and adequate picture of text-making skills.

Session One: Text-Making as Measured by Writer-Generated Editing. At the first session, children wrote the beginning of an invented story according to the instructions of an experimenter. They were asked to do the following: First, write a paragraph setting the scene for a made-up story. Second, proofread and make any changes in the setting paragraph. Third, write a second paragraph describing a main character. Fourth, proofread and make any changes in the character description. Fifth, write a paragraph telling about an initiating ("the first exciting") event in their story. Sixth, proofread the initiating event paragraph. At the end of each segment, the observer saved the text-generated-to-date in a new file. Once a child had made changes in the last paragraph, there was a short break in the session. Children and observer talked about stories that the children had read and liked, while a complete copy of the story was printed. Finally, children were asked to read over all they had written and to make it into a "good story." This final editing was done on hard copy, as suggested by pilot interviews in which children had said that they needed to see the text "all at once" (that is, not just screen segments one at a time) in order to do the final editing. Entire sessions were tape-recorded. Transcripts were prepared in which verbal comments and keyboard activity were interlaced.

Session Two: Text Making as Measured by Responses to Local Editing Tasks. In the second session, children's text-making abilities were probed. In this session, children were asked to make the kinds of editing changes that, in the work of adult writers, are likely to exercise and expose the author's ability to think in terms of connected text. The purpose was to find out whether first-session estimates of children's text-making abilities represented the full range of their skills. These probes consisted of requests for the types of radical changes that a writer can execute easily on a computer screen with word processing software. These changes included insertion of information and inversion of information. In the first case, children were asked to provide more detail in their story. If children could not spontaneously locate a place to do this, they were specifically asked to insert new information about a character and an event. In the second case, children were asked to try switching the position of two paragraphs in their story "to see if there is another, better way of telling the story." If children had difficulty with the task, they were asked to switch the setting and the character paragraphs. Both kinds of changes were presented to children as ways of making their stories more interesting and more effective. In each case, they were asked to execute the suggested editing and then to make whatever further changes they thought were needed. The new versions were each saved as separate files. Again, transcripts combining text entries, edits, and verbal comments were prepared and analyzed.

Session Three: Text Making as Measured by Wholesale Editing Tasks. In the third session, children were shown their original stories and asked to turn their original texts into a particular type or genre of story. The genre varied across the three data collection points (for example, a mystery story, an adventure tale, a funny story). Here, too, transcripts were prepared and analyzed.

Findings from Structured Editing Tasks

Taken together, students' responses to the structured editing tasks suggested a consistent, if tentative, picture of the ways in which the ability to sustain textual continuity varies across junior high school and high school writers. In the course of working on these editing tasks, younger and older writers displayed differences in the amounts of writing they treated as unified text, in the range of connections they sought to repair, and in the types of information and the locations where they could insert into their texts.

Local Versus Systematic Texts. In the structured editing sessions, children had to reorder and insert in such a way that the network of ties existing in their original texts was disrupted. Given their ages, it is not surprising that both younger and older children were aware of the most obvious occasions on which the fabric of their writing was torn apart (Cazden and Michaels, in press; Wolf and Pusch, in press). For example, when what had been the first sentence of a middle paragraph became the opening sentence in his story, one eleven-year-old writer reworked his references to character, setting, and time so that the sentence functioned as an appropriate introduction:

Original

Mick and Greg were now flying high over Bermuda

Revision

Mick and Greg, the two Bambinos brothers, were on vacation, flying over Bermuda.

Subsequently, the author corrected the sentence that had been demoted from being the first of the story to a position several paragraphs into the text:

Original

The two Bambinos brothers, Mick and Greg, had left Fargo, North Dakota far behind them.

Revision

Now that they were on vacation, Mick and Greg hardly even thought about their lives back home in Fargo, North Dakota.

Adolescent writers may write more elegantly, but their responses to this kind of postrevision text making were not qualitatively different. One fourteen-year-old reworked the sentence that had been moved to the opening of her story in the following way:

Original

She was never completely happy.

Revision

Ever since I knew her, Shira Calgary, my landlady, never seemed completely happy.

However, is was what happened following the initial stitching up of obvious ruptures that distinguished the performances of younger and older writers. While younger writers recognized and corrected at least some violations of the cumulative obligations of their texts, they provided little evidence that they thought in terms of a chain of problems that a local revision could cause throughout the text. In this regard, refer back to the Sylvester Hufflanger example cited earlier.

In comparison, older writers appeared to see the implications of a local change for later portions of their text, including portions beyond the immediate location of the initial revision. When they encountered a discontinuity in the text or decided to make a local edit, they often scrolled through their texts following the thread of that particular issue (such as reference terms or verb tenses). Alternatively, they continued to read through the text, entering the appropriate revision each time they came to a relevant instance. Thus, once the author of "Shira" changed the tense in one sentence, she read ahead to a series of later verbs, making parallel changes, until she was satisfied that she had come to a location where she knew the verbs were correct. Similarly, following the insertion of new text describing the main character as a vulnerable individual, the same adolescent writer moved through the text making a series of subtle word changes that sustained this portrait. For instance, when she narrated how the character had been put up for adoption, she made this series of edits:

Original

Shira went to a Children's Home.

Revision 1

Shira's mother put her in a Children's Home.

Revision 2

Shira and her twin were placed in a Children's Home.

In large part, the younger writers appeared to use a different editing process. They rarely commented on the consequences of current changes for later texts, or skimmed or scrolled through their texts, checking for consistency. Instead, younger writers read consecutively through their texts, making revisions only when they came upon glaring errors or discontinuities. The only exception to this general rule occurred when younger writers were asked to transform their original texts into another genre. This exception will be discussed later.

Narrow or Broad Repertoires of Connections. Across the various structured editing tasks, writers of different ages exhibited a concern for a different range or repertoire of textual changes. In comparison to younger writers, older writers displayed a sense that any one change may call for several different types of adjustments in the surrounding text. Younger writers seemed alert chiefly to ruptures in the continuity of reference terms and sequences of action. Thus, the eleven-year-old author of the story about Mick and Greg who inverted paragraphs revised instances in which a pronoun precedes its associated noun phrases, and he edited *also* when it suggested a prior action that did not occur until later in his story as revised.

Adolescent writers monitored a wider repertoire of textual connections. In particular, the high school writers monitored the compactness and the tone of their stories when they conducted large-scale revisions, particularly when they had made insertions and deletions. In the following revision, one adolescent writer added information to a previous paragraph. Then she went over the added text making several small changes that introduced a continuity of tone or texture with the prior material.

Original

All through her life, Shira Limnock (who was outwardly practically perfect) had been haunted by the vague and rather disconcerting feeling that some part of her was missing. At age 30, she was the landlady for several apartments downtown. She lived alone with her odd feeling of waiting for someone else to arrive, or maybe, return.

Revision

All through her life, Shira Limnock (who was outwardly practically perfect) had been haunted by the vague and rather disconcerting feeling that some part of her was missing. At age 30, she was the landlady for several apartments downtown.

Her   *but cold*

~~*The*~~ *apartments were very nice, rather large,*∧*with giant rooms and many windows. Originally Shira had occupied the entire fifth floor, but then she*

                     alone

decided that she really wanted to live∧*without worrying about her neighbors all the time, so she moved to a little house some distance away. So she lived alone with her odd feeling of waiting for someone else to arrive, or maybe, return.*

Extension Versus Expansion of Text. An additional dimension of the difference between younger and older writers' concepts of text emerged from analyses of the third writing session, when young writers were asked to turn a previously drafted story into a story of a different genre (for example, to make a mystery story out of it). Under this condition, eleven-year-olds conducted a series of revisions that spanned their entire texts. Thus, one eleven-year-old writer was able to take an "ordinary" story and turn it into an adventure tale by adding on an episode about a mysterious engine failure. In addition, he inserted such words as *suddenly, dangerous,* and *frightening.* He also added "tough-guy" dialogue at two points in the story. When younger writers added new events or sections of dialogue, they inserted the information only at the beginning or the end of the story or at paragraph boundaries within existing materials. The following example suggests the types and locations of additions typically introduced by preadolescent writers as they transformed their stories:

Original

Mick Bambinos and his brother Greg were flying over the Bermuda triangle.

Revision 1

Mick Bambinos and his brother Greg were flying over the Bermuda triangle when suddenly the engine stopped. Mick lunged at the c.b. and tried to radio to the nearest airport. But his response was only static. The plane was falling hundreds of feet per second and Greg was panicking because the parachutes were tangled. Mick swerved out of the triangle and as if by magic the engine started working.

Revision 2

Mick Bambinos and his brother Greg were flying over the Bermuda triangle when suddenly the engine stopped. Mick lunged at the c.b. and tried to radio to the nearest airport. But his response was only static. The plane was falling hundreds of feet per second and Greg was panicking because the parachutes were tangled. Mick swerved out of the triangle and as if by magic the engine started working. A noise came from the c.b. We read you loud and clear. Are you there? Roger.

In contrast, high school–age writers asked to make the same kinds of transformations introduced substantial changes in the midstream of their texts. They were as likely to insert or delete information at the start or the middle of a paragraph as at the end. While older writers sometimes introduced novel events, they just as often thickened or embroidered the events originally mentioned. In this regard, refer back to the example in which the adolescent writer inserts a description of Shira Limnock's apartments.

Findings from Spontaneous Writing

At one level, the pattern of revisions was remarkably the same in younger and older writers during spontaneous writing sessions. Across both age groups, three levels of spontaneous revision occurred. The simplest type of revision, in-stream editing, looked remarkably similar in both junior high school and high school writers. As these authors wrote their narratives, they caught and fixed such obvious mistakes as typing and spelling errors and the occasional omission of words or punctuation. In other words, without explicit revision time or prompting, "line editing" (Graves, 1978) was the rule. Even when proofreading their narratives, both groups of writers confined themselves largely to upgrades at the level of individual words or phrases. Thus, a younger writer makes the following revisions:

Original

They went to Bermuda. As they were flying through Bermuda...

Revision

They went to Bermuda thanks to a generous gift from their parents. As they were flying over Bermuda...

Older writers made two other types of minor revision. First, they deleted words and phrases in order to make their writing more compact:

Original

Shira was the same at six years of age, as at twelve years of age, as at twenty-five years of age.

Revision

Shira was the same at six, at twelve and at twenty-five.

Second, the older writers attempted some within-sentence reorderings:

Original

Ever since her twin was adopted, Shira had the impression that something was missing.

Revision

Shira carried around the impression that some part of her was missing, ever since her twin was adopted.

However, there were aspects of unstructured editing behavior that extended the differences in text making evident from younger and older writers' responses to the structured editing tasks. In the context of spontaneous writing, preadolescents treated their stories as a series of local texts. For example, if a younger writer changed tense in one part of a sentence, he was likely to make a parallel change in the rest of the sentence yet fail to check the remainder of the text. Efforts to follow particular syntactic threads were particularly vulnerable if the younger writer stumbled across a second kind of revision while working on the first. In the following example, an eleven-year-old began by fixing tenses, encountered a false reference to an earlier event, fixed that, and then failed to resume editing tenses.

Original

Mick started grabbing the controls and takes the parachutes which also frightened Greg who yells "Be careful you fool!!!"

Revision

Mick grabbed the controls and took the parachutes which frightened Greg who yells "Be careful you fool!!!"

In addition, the unstructured writing sessions included telling instances of writers' stumbling on good ideas midstream. In the case of the younger writers, once a new idea occurred, they were often able to continue the change in subsequent text. Thus, part way through his story, one of the younger writers hit on the idea of making one of the two brothers in his story a comical character. From then on, he provided that character with wisecracks and exaggerated actions. However, he gave no evidence of considering the implications of his idea for the prior portion of his story. He simply left earlier appearances of the character untouched. By way of contrast, listen to this adolescent writer reflect on the consequences of having a new idea midstream:

> I had the idea of Shira as a perfectionist landlady in my head for a long time. I think I even tried a story about her in third grade. When I came here to do this writing project, I didn't have any good ideas, so I just plugged in my old Shira idea. That got me through the first paragraph. But then you asked for more . . . so I borrowed this idea about two separated twins from a book I read, *Herbert Rowbarge,* and I wrote the part about Shira being a twin who was left behind in a children's home when her sister was adopted. But there was no connection to the landlady part, so I had to go back to the beginning to include the idea of Shira's being only half a person. That's why I put in the sentences about Shira's feeling like something was missing.

As a result of her reflections, the author rewrote the first paragraphs of her text, inserting the idea of Shira's being incomplete at two early points in the introduction.

Original

At age 30, Shira was the landlady for several apartments downtown. The apartments were very nice, rather large, with giant rooms and many windows. Originally, Shira herself had occupied the entire fifth floor, but then she decided that she really wanted to live without worrying about her neighbors all the time, so she moved to a little house some distance away.

With the exception of physical features, Shira had been the same all through her life. She had always been a perfectionist, and had always appeared two or three steps ahead of everyone else.

Revision

All through her life, Shira Limnock (who was outwardly practically perfect) had been haunted by the vague and rather disconcerting feeling that some part of her was missing. At age 30, she was the landlady for several apartments downtown. The apartments were very nice, rather large, with giant rooms and many windows. Originally Shira had occupied the entire fifth floor, but slowly she decided that she wanted to live without worrying about her neighbors, so she moved into a little house some distance away. So she lived alone with her odd feeling of waiting for someone else to arrive, or maybe, return.

With the exception of physical features, Shira had been the same all through her life. She had always been a perfectionist and had always appeared two or three steps ahead of everyone else, trying to stifle the inner sense that something was missing inside herself.

For experienced adolescent writers, this continuity principle operated in the opposite direction as well. The same adolescent commented:

It's a pain, but when you cut out something, you have to go all the way back and cut out all the times you mentioned it, and worse, you have to get out all the things that build on it, too.

In her first draft, this writer included details in her description of the main character, Shira, that suggested a witchlike, almost cruel, streak: "She had long red nails." "Her favorite color was green so dark it looked black." As the writer continued to work on her text, the Shira character evolved from the original landlady, becoming an abandoned twin. Following her addition of the material about Shira's being left alone, the writer scrolled through her text deleting the sentences and phrases that depicted a harsher character.

Conclusion

The research on writing and revision indicates that a major difference between skilled and unskilled writers lies in the way in which they edit their texts (Beach, 1976; Sommers, 1978). Poor writers appear to make changes only at the word level, whereas better writers consider the overall effect of their document, inserting and deleting large segments of text before combing the sentences for word-level errors. The observations presented here not only confirm but extend this characterization of writing skill.

Indeed, one critical difference between more and less sophisticated writers has to do with the widening of the window of writing that they can consider as connected text. In their writing and subsequent editing, junior high school students sometimes drop the thread as they write and edit at various locations through their texts. They may shift tenses or lose hold of the tonality of a narrative as they move from paragraph to paragraph.

However, it is too simple to characterize the differences between the junior high school and high school writers in terms of the sheer amount of writing that they can successfully treat as text. Preadolescent and adolescent writers differ also in the range of cohesive ties that they attempt to create and monitor throughout a narrative. Thus, unlike a younger writer, the author of the Shira story scrolls through her text attending to the tone of the story and to the verb tenses simultaneously.

A final dimension in the development of text-making abilities is the appearance of the capacity to expand rather than simply to extend text. When younger writers are asked to insert additional story material, they typically add material at the beginning, at the end, or at subdivision boundaries within their narratives. Moreover, they usually add new events or dialogue instead of expanding on existing events. In contrast, adolescent writers add material at any number of points within the text. Older writers insert text that thickens the portrayal of individual events and that often multiplies the ties to earlier portions of the text.

Taken together, the observations of elicited and spontaneous revision indicate a shift in skilled writers' ability to create coherent texts between the ages of eleven and fifteen. Perhaps this development can be summarized as a move away from the concatenation of a series of short, local texts toward the construction of one continuous text network bound together along any number of axes. Such findings echo those of earlier work on composition. Thus, word- and sentence-level writing by college freshmen has been described as practically flawless. Nevertheless, their essays lack the kind of consistent connectedness required for coherent arguments or narratives (Cooper and others, 1979).

Stepping back from developmental findings, we can note that the writing and editing performances described here raise questions about how we teach students to think about texts, regardless of the writing medium, if writers are going to be successful at writing coherent texts in which later elements build efficiently on earlier information. It is a demanding task to generate carefully connected prose: Issues of the presentation of required information, syntactic ties, and semantic links must all be juggled. In addition, as writers revise, reorderings, deletions, and shifts in emphasis further stress their ability to produce smoothly and adequately connected text.

52

Currently, microcomputer technology places the raw capacity for large-scale editing squarely within the reach of many writers. However, the sheer existence of such options hardly guarantees that they will be used thoughtfully. The observations presented earlier indicate that large-scale editing may involve several skills over and above those required for proofreading. The low incidence and simplicity of most spontaneous editing suggests that it is an achievement to think about revisions that involve deletion, insertion, or reordering. Even in structured editing tasks in which specific large-scale revisions are requested, additional skills are required in order to execute revisions smoothly, restoring or even improving the connections within the text. Hence, both software designers and teachers must consider doing much more than simply making word processing software available. They have to discover ways of teaching students to think in terms of large-scale changes and to make such changes with an eye on the resulting ripples of effects throughout their texts.

The author and writing teacher John Gardner (1984) advised his students that changing the name of the protagonist "shakes the floor" under a whole story. This shaking is both problematic and promising. If writers are not taught to think about the text as a network of meanings, many of them will never write effectively across sentence boundaries. However, if writers can master such interconnections within texts, they have the tools needed to build arguments or write compelling narratives. Consequently, an outstanding question is how to harness the capacities of microprocessors so that a wide range of writers can discover what Tolstoy (quoted in Bertoff, 1978, p. 252) knew about composition: It involves "the ability to combine what follows with what precedes, all the while keeping in mind what is already written down."

References

Beach, R. "Self-Evaluation Strategies of Extensive Revisers and Nonrevisers." *College Composition and Communication,* 1976, *27,* 160–164.
Bertoff, A. "Tolstoy, Vygotsky, and the Making of Meaning." *College Composition and Communication,* 1978, *29,* 249–255.
Cazden, C., and Michaels, S. "Spontaneous Repairs in Sharing Time Narratives: The Intersection of Metalinguistic Awareness, Speech Event, and Narrative Style." In S. W. Freedman (Ed.), *The Acquisition of Written Language: Revision and Response.* Norwood, N.J.: Ablex, in press.
Cooper, C., Cherry, R., Gerber, R., Fleisher, S., Copley, B., and Sartisky, M. *Writing Abilities of Regularly Admitted Freshmen at SUNY–Buffalo.* New York: SUNY Learning Center, 1979.
Daiute, C. Presentation to the Principals Center. Graduate School of Education, Harvard University, Cambridge, Mass., October 1984.
Gardner, H. "Children's Literary Development: The Realms of Metaphors and Stories." In P. McGhee and A. Chapman (Eds.), *Children's Humour.* New York: Wiley, 1980.

Gardner, J. *The Art of Fiction.* New York: Knopf, 1984.

Graves, D. H. *Balance the Basics: Let Them Write.* New York: Ford Foundation, 1978.

Greenfield, P. M. *Mind and Media: The Effects of Television, Video Games, and Computers.* Cambridge, Mass.: Harvard University Press, 1984.

Halliday, M. A. K., and Hasan, R. *Cohesion in English.* London: Longman, 1976.

Inhelder, B., and Piaget, J. *The Growth of Logical Thinking from Childhood to Adolescence.* New York: Basic Books, 1958.

Jarrell, R. *Jerome: The Biography of a Poem.* New York: Grossman, 1971.

Kress, G. *Learning to Write.* London: Routledge & Kegan Paul, 1982.

Mandler, J. *Stories, Scripts, and Scenes: Aspects of Schema Theory.* Hillsdale, N.J.: Erlbaum, 1984.

Mandler, J. M., and Johnson, N. S. "Remembrance of Things Parsed: Story Structure and Recall." *Cognitive Psychology,* 1977, *9,* 111-151.

Marr, D. *Vision: A Computational Investigation into the Human Representation and Processing of Information.* San Francisco: W. H. Freeman, 1984.

Nelson, K., and Gruendel, J. M. "At Morning, It's Lunchtime: A Scriptal View of Children's Dialogues." *Discourse Processes,* 1979, *2,* 73-94.

Nold, E. W. "Revising." In C. H. Frederiksen and J. F. Dominic (Eds.), *Writing: The Nature, Development, and Teaching of Written Communication.* Vol. 2. Hillsdale, N.J.: Erlbaum, 1981.

Papert, S. *Mindstorms: Children, Computers, and Powerful Ideas.* New York: Basic Books, 1980.

Perkins, D. *The Mind's Best Work.* Cambridge, Mass.: Harvard University Press, 1981.

Rumelhart, D. E. "Notes on a Schema for Stories." In D. Bobrow and A. Collins (Eds.), *Representation and Understanding: Studies in Cognitive Science.* New York: Academic Press, 1975.

Salomon, G. "Television Is 'Easy' and Print Is 'Tough': The Differential Investment of Mental Effort in Learning as a Function of Perceptions and Attributions." *Journal of Educational Psychology,* in press.

Schank, R., and Abelson, R. *Scripts, Plans, Goals, and Understandings.* Hillsdale, N.J.: Erlbaum, 1977.

Slackman, E. "Filling in the Gaps: Inferential Processes in Children's Comprehension of Oral Discourse." Paper presented at the Boston University Child Language Conference, Boston, Mass., October 1984.

Sommers, N. "Revision Strategies of Experienced Writers and Student Writers." Unpublished address to a meeting of the Modern Language Association, December 1978.

Turkle, S. *The Intimate Machine.* New York: Basic Books, 1984.

van Dijk, T. A. *Some Aspects of Text Grammars.* The Hague: Mouton, 1972.

Wolf, D., and Pusch, J. "The Origins of Autonomous Texts in Play Boundaries." In L. Galda and A. Pellegrini (Eds.), *Play, Language, and Story: The Development of Children's Literate Behavior.* Norwood, N.J.: Ablex, in press.

Dennis P. Wolf is a research associate at the Harvard Graduate School of Education, where she directs a study of the transition from early symbolic skills to literate symbol use.

The presentation of visual and spatial information in an interactive format with computer graphics makes the computer a unique tool for experiences with imagery and for developing knowledge about space.

Computer Graphics, Visual Imagery, and Spatial Thought

Elisa L. Klein

As the computer becomes commonplace in the world of children, questions are being asked about its impact on development. Does the computer environment offer anything distinctive that will influence developmental processes? Greenfield (1984) and others have suggested that, as a medium of communication like print or television, computers will eventually play a significant role in the child's acquisition of literacy. Papert (1980) argues that the computer has potential for influencing cognition at an early age by providing a powerful environment for the development of logical and abstract thought. In Chapter Two of this volume, Forman speculates on the development of a new symbolism known as kinetic print, in which the child interacts with a type of active iconic symbol. In Chapter One of this volume, Chaillé and Littman discuss the benefits of computer simulation for the child's testing of theories about the physical world.

At issue is the fundamental role of the computer in the child's construction of knowledge. Is the computer such a powerful object as to

I would like to thank Stephen Acker, Patti Baker, George Forman, Susan Golbeck, and Barbara Kienzle for their helpful comments on earlier versions of this chapter. The research reported here was supported in part by grants from the Ohio State University College of Education and the Spencer Foundation.

E. L. Klein (Ed.). *Children and Computers.* New Directions for Child Development, no. 28. San Francisco: Jossey-Bass, June 1985.

actually change the structure of children's thought? Or, as Glick (1983) contends, is the computer a *tool* that will change the way in which children look at the world but not necessarily change thought itself? Glick finds little evidence in the research on computer–child interaction to support the radical change suggested by the first conceptualization. Rather, the computer may provide a unique way to be introduced to and interact with objects and events in the world:

> The original conceptualization likened the computer as a highly structured stimulus environment whose structures would eventually occasion changes in the cognitive and social structure of [children]. Ultimately, some form of isomorphism between computer and [child] procedural rules was expected.
>
> A revised view. . . [The] computer is not regarded as a structure, but rather as a tool. The focus is on the new things in the world that can be revealed (perhaps uniquely) by the computer as tool. Thus, rather than being the topic of cognition, the computer is seen as its tool. In this view, the computer becomes a source of new kinds of information, revealing nonobvious features of our experienced world, much in the way that a microscope might open up hitherto unimagined worlds [Glick, 1983, p. 60].

In this chapter, I will explore the potential influence of the "computer as tool" on one aspect of cognition, the development of imagery and spatial thought. The presentation of important visual and spatial information, such as rotations, transformations, enlargements, and so forth, in an interactive format makes the computer a unique tool for experiences with imagery and for the development of knowledge about space.

The presentation and manipulation of visual and spatial information on the computer is distinctive from other media forms, such as video and text. As such, working with this information may require a different level of symbolic understanding on the part of the user. Thus, a secondary theme of this chapter is a comparison of the computer with other media in the presentation of spatial and visual data.

The chapter starts with a discussion of how children's interactions with computer graphics may influence the development of imagery and spatial skills. (Unless otherwise noted, the term *computer graphics* refers to graphics created on a microcomputer, not on a mainframe computer.) Evidence is scarce, since this is a relatively new area of research; examples come from the literature on educational applications and from research on children's interactions with video games. In the next section, I examine the varying symbolic requirements of the computer as compared with other media. The last section shows how computer graphics can be used to examine traditional imagery questions.

Computer as Enhancer and Illustrator

Imagery is used as an aid in a variety of cognitive processes; as a representational aid in memory (Kosslyn, 1980; Piaget and Inhelder, 1973), in abstraction, prediction, and hypothetico-deductive reasoning. The ability to manipulate images mentally, such as in rotations or transformations, is essential for such spatially oriented subject matter as mathematics, geography, and other natural sciences and for the arts, particularly those involving three-dimensional presentations, such as dance and sculpture. Liben (1981, p. 12), defines spatial thought as "thinking that concerns or makes use of space in some way. Spatial thought is knowledge that individuals have access to, can reflect upon, or can manipulate, as in spatial problem solving or spatial imagery." Obviously, this type of thinking is critical for such common activities as reading a map, giving verbal directions for how to get from one place to another, or creating an image of one's home and walking through the rooms in order to determine where one left a missing set of keys.

Although we think of computer graphics as a relatively new phenomenon, they have been used for well over a decade as an instructional aid (Hammond, 1971). Complex concepts once presented in strictly a verbal mode or in a two-dimensional, static graphic display can now be augmented and expanded with computer simulations (Hortin, 1982; Bork, 1979). Animation, simulation, and other graphic capabilities have been used in engineering (Pleck, 1975; Wozny, 1978), physics (diSessa, 1982 and Chapter Six in this volume; Hughes, 1974), and mathematics (Hooper, 1982; Wegman, 1974). Some computer graphics techniques may be more useful than others for specific content. LOGO, a computer language with a strong graphics component (Papert, 1980), has been shown to be useful for learning spatial and mathematical concepts, such as geometry. With LOGO, children develop a "turtle" geometry, in which they direct the cursor (a turtle) around the spatial environment of the screen in order to create objects. As they give the turtle directions, children manipulate geometric concepts. For example, the difference between giving the turtle the direction to move R90 and R360 is the difference between a right angle and a full rotation.

In a small exploratory study, Cambre (1983) examined how

different types of animation and presentation styles might affect performance on a problem involving the concept of volume. In addition, the effect of field dependence and field independence (as measured by the Embedded Figures Test) on performance was assessed. College students viewed one of three different animation sequences in which a cube doubles in volume. Volume is represented by eight smaller cubes, which fit into the original cube. In each of the animation sequences, the cube is manipulated and turned through space as it is enlarged. The smaller cubes "dance" in and out of the large cube to show the increased volume. In condition one, subjects viewed a commercially prepared cell animation (the traditional animation technique used in cartooning), in which the cube was opaque white on a blue background. In condition two, the animation was a computer-generated monochrome "wireframe" animation (only the outlines of the cubes were presented) of the content of the commercial film. In condition three, a full-color computer-generated replication of the original film was used; each of the smaller cubes was a different opaque color. Cambre found that the full-color animation sequence used in condition three elicited the best-elaborated verbal descriptions of the task as well as the best comprehension for all subjects. The contextually richer animation sequence in condition three appeared to enhance performance. It was also found that field-dependent subjects were more successful in condition three than they were in conditions one and two.

Graphics and animation techniques have been used to create and represent art and to enhance art instruction (Csuri, 1974, 1977). Computer graphics is now taught in regular courses in university art, art education, and architecture departments. Creating an image on the computer screen enables the artist or architect to manipulate components of the image, to rotate the image for perspective, to enlarge or reduce certain sections, and to change color, shading, and pattern much more easily than when working directly in the medium (such as paint, wood, metal, or plaster). The computer itself has become an artistic medium. Art created with computer graphics is now being presented at shows and in galleries. (Most of this art is created on sophisticated mainframe computers that have high-quality high-resolution graphics capabilities. While the resolution and detail available with microcomputer graphics have improved tremendously, they are still not of the quality available on larger, more powerful computers.)

Computer graphics may be an especially useful medium for representing art that involves movement, such as dance. Savage and Officer (1978) describe the implementation of CHOREO, an interactive computer graphics model for learning and interpreting dance notation (both Labanotation and the Massine notation method). Dance notation is an important method for permanently representing a pattern of movement. Until Labanotation was developed, there was no real universal method for preserving choreography. In the traditional Labanotation method, the complex positions of different parts of the dancer's body are captured in a notation system that details such important information as angle of position, relation to other body parts, duration of position, direction of position, height of position, and relation to the beat of the musical score.

The actual dance itself can, of course, be captured on film. Dancers as well as athletes often use videotapes to analyze performance. However, while film gives a sense of the whole that dance notation cannot, it is limited in its ability to break the performance down into individual steps, which dance notation can do. The great choreographer George Balanchine (1970, p. xi–xii) summarized the problem in these words: "While some people advocate the use of films to record ballet, I have found them useful only in indicating the style of the finished product and in suggesting the general overall visual picture and staging. A film cannot reproduce a dance step by step, since the lens shoots from but one angle and there is a general confusion of blurred impressions which even constant re-showing can never eliminate. Labanotation records the *structure* of a dance, revealing with perfect clarity each of the specific movements of each performer."

Film, then, gives an overall picture but does not adequately or accurately record the specific features of the dance. The CHOREO interactive computer program extends the traditional notation method by the ease with which it is learned and by its storage, simulation, and playback capacities. CHOREO, which uses Massine notation as its base, allows the user to depict key body positions with an actual graphic model of a dancer. While motional commands, such as jumps, runs, or walks, were not developed for the original program, the user can replay a sequence of stationary movements. The user begins by selecting key body part positions from a main menu. Submenus subsequently direct the user to define the finer levels of information about the position, such as the relationship of the position to other body parts, the height of position, and so on. CHOREO–L transposes the symbol system developed for Labanotation onto the computer. The user selects the particular Laban symbol by touching a pen to an acoustic tablet. An interactive graphics system, such as CHOREO, combined with a videotape of the actual performance, thus gives both a micro as well as a macro view of the dance. The differential capacities of video and computer will again be compared in a discussion of research on imagery later in this chapter.

Spatial and Visual Skills and Video Games. The popularity of video games has on the whole been rather short-lived. Media attention to the impact of video games on the child and the community has faded as the sale of home video games and arcade attendance have decreased dramatically. Yet the tremendous allure of video games for children and young adults has been the subject of several studies. What makes the games so motivating? Malone (1980, 1981) reports the results of a series of studies about the types of games that children enjoy and suggests that challenge, fantasy, and curiosity are the three factors that provide the greatest source of intrinsic motivation. In one study, children from kindergarten through eighth grade were asked about their preferences for different computer games and about game features that were the most important in determining their preferences. Games with goals were the most preferred. While visual effects were considered to be important, children viewed them as less important than audio effects. Overall, however, graphic games were much more popular than word games. As Greenfield (1984, pp. 99–100) reports, "graphics games such as Petball (computer pinball) and Snake 2 (two players controlling motion and shooting of snakes) were more popular than word games such as Eliza (conversation with a simulated psychiatrist) and Gold (a fill-in-the-blanks story about Goldilocks). A clue as to the attraction of *moving* visual images comes from the fact that the three most unpopular graphics games—Stars, Snoopy, and Draw—have no animation at all or much less than more popular games."

While the visual quality of the game certainly makes it attractive, animation alone is not the primary source of motivation. As already show, the accomplishment of a clearly defined goal is what makes video games exciting. This interactive capacity enables children to become, as Greenfield notes, "personally involved" and sets video games apart from more passive activities, such as television watching: "Video games are the first medium to combine visual dynamism with an active participatory role for the child" (Greenfield, 1984, p. 101).

Within the interactive environment of the video game, what do children learn? Spatial skills are important for successful participation in many of the games (Greenfield, 1984; Lowery and Knirk (1982–1983). For example, locomotor skills and route knowledge are critical to such games as PacMan. Often, three-dimensional information is simulated on the video screen, requiring the player to manipulate perspective. Lowery and Knirk (1982–1983, pp. 160, 162) note that the coordination of horizontal and vertical axes is often implicit in such games as Space Invaders, which "require[s] that the player repeatedly determine the location of both the vertical 'Invaders' and the horizontally moving cursor, representing the player, while at the same time anticipat[ing] the intersection points of imaginary lines."

The coordination of horizontal and vertical axes is not just the province of video games; it is also required for various rudimentary types of programming. For example, to create a simple picture using the graphics mode in BASIC, the user builds blocks of color and shape by identifying the horizontal and vertical coordinates on the screen. In an exploration of children's interactions with computers, fifth-grade children used this procedure to create static and animated graphics. At the conclusion of the project, the children were asked about what they had learned from working with the computer. An almost unanimous response had to do with the procedure involved in estimating points on the horizontal and vertical axes.

As video games decrease in popularity, will the opportunities to use spatial manipulations in a gaming context also disappear? I do not think so, because children now have available to them a whole new range of computer capabilities that involve increased interaction, more self-initiated programming, and higher levels of problem solving. In many of these activities, the child is the creator of the action and as such the one who must manipulate and transform the images. Several of these activities are mentioned by Forman in Chapter Two of this volume. For instance, with the Smurf Paint and Play Workshop, children can animate their own drawings or move previously created characters with the aid of an animation package. In this type of activity, the child must use spatial representation to decide where and how the character is going to move, how to coordinate the movements of two or more characters, and so forth. These skills may be even more critical for activities like Pinball Construction Set, where the child must think through a whole series of actions (and determine the consequences of those actions) in order to create the pinball game.

Tools, Techniques, and Tricks of the Trade. The purpose of any tool is to enable the user to perform an action or attain an objective with increased ease and flexibility or in an enhanced fashion. Information is transmitted efficiently, and important features of the information are highlighted or pinpointed in some way. In this section, I will summarize some of the techniques and capacities of the computer that are especially helpful in understanding spatial relationships. These techniques are in accord with Glick's (1983) notion of the computer as a tool that helps to illustrate important features of the child's world. The question is, What can the computer do that is unique?

The brief review of educational applications in the preceding section shows that computer graphics can indeed enhance, pinpoint, and extend spatial information encountered in the "real" world. In addition, graphics, simulation, and animation can be used to provide views of the world that are not usually available yet that are essential in understanding certain types of spatial relationships and in creating certain types of imagery. For example, Shepard and Metzler (1971) and others have studied mental rotation as an important form of spatial imagery. *Rotations* of objects and scenes can be accomplished with many computer graphics programs and with certain peripherals, such as graphics pads and touch screens. Transformational imagery (Dean, 1976; Klein and Liben, 1981; Piaget and Inhelder, 1971) is a means for representing the changes in the form or shape of an object or event. Piaget (1977) has noted that reflecting on transformations is critical to constructing knowledge. *Transformations* of objects are easily represented through *animation*. The transformations can be slowed, accelerated, compared with other transformations, and enlarged to show particular detail. Later on in this chapter, I will summarize a study in which computer graphics were used to create transformational imagery problems.

Besides the animation, rotation, transformation, *enlargement, slow motion,* and *fast motion* techniques just mentioned, other computer capabilities may enhance or extend the child's view of the spatial world. Clearly, *three-dimensional simulation* is a critical capability. So is *stop action,* which allows the child to stop the motion or animation temporarily in order to view a particular motion and then to replay the scene as many times as desired. Both Chaillé and Littman in Chapter One and Forman in Chapter Two speculate on the use of *action trails,* which allow the child to reflect on a whole series of actions and to compare two or more different strings of actions.

Implicit in all these techniques is the concept of *interaction,* which may prove to be the most important "trick of the trade." In the computer environment, the child is constantly receiving feedback from and giving feedback to the display on the screen. Creations and manipulations are continuously added to, changed, played back, and rearranged. This activity, in which the child becomes caught up in a dynamic conversation with his or her own creation, sets the computer apart from many other instructional methods, from other games, and from television. As such, it may provide an important means for constructing knowledge about the self and the world.

Computer as Medium

How is the computer distinct from other media? Is the symbolic level different from that of television? Is information that is communicated through the medium of the computer different from information communicated through other iconic or analogic systems? Research on the transmittal of structurally equivalent information by different types of media has primarily involved comparisons of film or television with print (Baggett, 1979; Char and Merigoff, 1981; Chatman, 1980; Meringoff and others, 1983). The focus of many of these studies has been on the child's comprehension of information, such as facts or descriptive characteristics, or the inferring of thoughts, feelings, mood, or intentions (Meringoff and others, 1983). Other researchers have examined the impact of particular techniques, such as sound effects, music, or editing (Char and Meringoff, 1981) on comprehension and recall.

Salomon (1974, 1979), Olson and Bruner (1974) and others have suggested that the distinctions between different media rest not so much on the technology itself but on the nature of the symbol system inherent in the medium. Thus, when comparing comprehension of information presented in different media, researchers need to be sure that the content of the message is as similar as possible. What varies is the manner in which the content is presented. In the research just mentioned, there are some major differences between the symbol systems involved; for example, language predominates in text, while graphics and movement predominate in film and television. Even though there is some overlap in the method of presentation (there are pictures in the storybook, and both the story and the film involve a spoken text), the overall packaging of the information is dissimilar.

These differences may not be as obvious when we examine information delivered via computer or video. However, while there are many similarities between the two media (both are presented on the same television-monitor, both use pictures as the dominant symbol system, and both symbol systems are active rather than static), there are some important distinctions that may require differential processing on the part of the learner. The most important distinction relates to the level of symbolic abstraction involved. With video, the image is concrete, and it is clear that the taped events are real. With the computer, the actions depicted are analogs of the actual event. The graphics are created symbols that often are very different from what one would see on film. For instance, the action may be represented in a cartoon-like format using stick figures. Of course, the level of abstraction depends in large part on the quality of the graphics and the animation, and on the skill of the programmer. However, with the type of software available in most educational settings and to most developmental researchers, the graphics tend to be more pictographic and abstract than lifelike.

Given the relatively recent emergence of computers, it is not surprising that there has been little research comparing them with other media. Moreover, the unique capabilities of the computer lead to a different range of questions and comparisons. The most obvious are the interactive capabilities, which enable the user to control and manipulate the information involved. The learner moves from being a passive recipient of information to becoming an active participant. For instance, in the research on story comprehension just mentioned, the child could actually control the outcome of the story, which could have a strong impact on comprehension, recall, or both. These interactive capabilities would be especially useful for problems in which the child was asked to generate a solution (or set of solutions) to a specific question. New responses could easily be compared with previous solutions, and responses could be altered without losing important information. The research described in the following section was designed specifically to compare computers with video; it addresses the interactive capabilities of both computer and video as well as the varying levels of symbols used in the different media.

Using Computer Graphics to Assess Imagery

In this section, I review a research study related to two issues presented earlier in this chapter: the imagery abilities of children and young adults in interactions with computer graphics, and computer and video as media for the presentation of visual and spatial information. This study, conducted with my colleague Stephen Acker (Acker and Klein, in press; Klein and Acker, 1984), was designed to examine how children and young adults address and solve identical imagery problems presented in two different media, real-life (that is, taped event) video and computer-generated graphic analogs. If the two media do indeed have different levels of symbolic requirements, then the differences should be reflected in performance. To test for these differences, we asked ninety-eight subjects at three grade and age levels (thirty third graders, thirty-six middle and high schoolers, and thirty-two college students) to complete a series of video and computer tasks involving anticipatory kinetic and transformational imagery. Kinetic imagery is used to represent objects as they move through space, such as the rotation of a rod through ninety degrees. Transformational imagery is used to represent the changes in the shape or form of an object, such as the extension of an arc or an angle into a straight line.

Parallel messages were developed using computer graphic and video representations of information required to solve a set of imagery problems. The point of departure was a set of tasks developed by Piaget and Inhelder (1971) and used by others (Dean, 1976; Klein and Liben, 1981) to assess levels of imagery ability. For this study, the tasks were embedded stories in which the main objective was to complete the anticipated but unseen movement of an object or the anticipated but unseen transformation of an event. Video and computer-animated graphic sequences were produced for each task. The video sequences used real actors in real settings. SuperPILOT, a Pascal-based language, was used in the computer sequences to create animated character analogs.

The steps required to complete each story task were parallel for the video and the computer forms. The video sequences were presented on a video editing machine, where frame-by-frame movement could be controlled by both the researcher and the subject. Subjects estimated the end state placement required to complete the story by making a mark on the monitor with a fiber tip pen. Following the prediction, the sequence was completed using slow motion so that the subject could clearly see the actual transformation. In the computer sequences, subjects estimated the end state by moving the point on the screen with a game paddle. Once the subject was satisfied with the estimate, the transformation was completed, and a program subroutine calculated the percentage and absolute error of the subject's response. In both video and computer tasks, estimates could be changed as many times as desired before answers were locked in. For the computer task, this was done via a loop through the interactive section of the routine. For the video task, this was done by erasing the marks with an alcohol swab, rewinding the tape, and playing it again.

Three imagery tasks were used. The traditional rod rotation kinetic imagery task, in which a rod is rotated through ninety degrees, was embedded in a story of a carpenter about to hit a nail with a hammer (Figure 1). Subjects were asked to create a visual image of where the nail should be in order to be hit by the hammer and then to move the nail to that point. In the second task, an arc is transformed into a straight line. The story is about a woman hanging a clothesline between a tree and a pole (Figure 2). The arc is thus stretched to its straight-line length. Here, subjects were asked to anticipate where the pole should be in order for the clothesline to be taut and then to move the pole to that point. In the third task, a forty-five-degree angle is transformed into a straight line. The story is about a cheerleader moving from a standing position into a full split (Figure 3). Once again, the angle is stretched to a straight-line position. Subjects were asked to anticipate where the cheerleader's right foot should be in order for the full split to be completed and then to move the foot to that point.

Several results are important to this discussion. In an analysis of variance with repeated measures, no significant main effects were

Figure 1. Original Kinetic Imagery Task and Created Story Problem: The Hammer

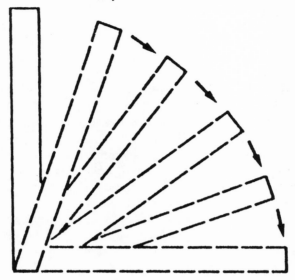

Kinetic imagery: rod rotation

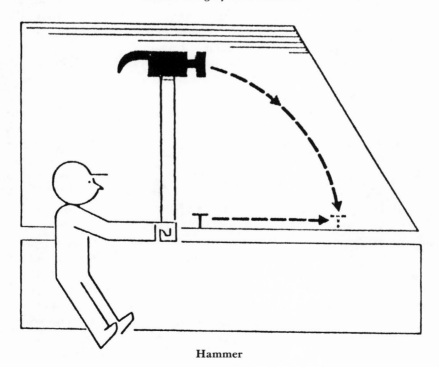

Hammer

Figure 2. Original Transformational Imagery Task and Created Story Problem: The Clothesline

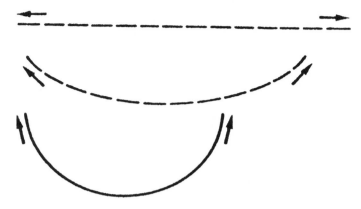

Transformational imagery: arc transformation

Clothesline

Figure 3. Original Transformational Imagery Task and Created Story Problem: The Cheerleader

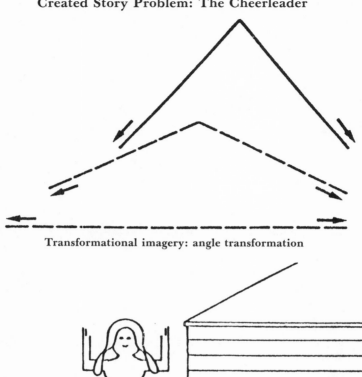

Transformational imagery: angle transformation

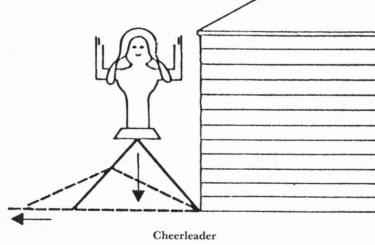

Cheerleader

found for age, type of task (kinetic or transformational), or mode (computer or video). While older children and young adults were more accurate overall than younger children, the differences with respect to age were not as great as one might expect given the wide range tested. However, there were significant interactions for age and grade level by mode and for mode by specific task. Post hoc tests revealed that performance was significantly better for the two oldest groups on computer tasks than on video tasks. The youngest subjects performed better on the video tasks, although the difference was not statistically significant. For the mode-by-task interaction, performance was more accurate on the computer version of the two transformational tasks (clothesline and cheerleader) than on the video version. Finally, there was a significant interaction for age and grade by task, with the youngest subjects demonstrating better performance on the cheerleader task than on the clothesline or hammer task.

Overall, performance was better on computer versions of the imagery tasks, particularly for older subjects. Moreover, performance was more accurate on the computer versions of the transformational imagery tasks than on the video versions. Transformational imagery was considered by Piaget and Inhelder (1971) to be more difficult than kinetic imagery, because it requires the complex coordination of changes in two dimensions, which kinetic imagery does not.

One explanation for the media differences in performance has to do with the ease and accessibility of the self-correcting loop on the computer. Subjects were able to change their initial estimate as many times as they wished without assistance. The text asked subjects whether they were satisfied with their end state placement. If not, pressing the *N* key promptly rerouted the program back to the beginning of the estimation phase, and subjects could move the object again. This procedure was not nearly as researcher-free on the video version. First, the query regarding accuracy came from the researcher, not from text on the video screen. If subjects were not satisfied with their initial placement, the correction had to be made by erasing the mark with alcohol, which the researcher had to supply, and then making a new mark. The overall control of the correction procedure was not as firmly in the hands of the subject as it was for the computer task. Some of these limitations would, of course, be eliminated with interactive videotape or videodisc. However, the cost of the initial hardware, the expense of producing videodiscs or interactive videotape, and the difficulty of obtaining a sharp freeze-frame image by amateurs make these options less practical. The interactive and recursive capabilities of the microcomputer are examples of the ways in which this tool, as Glick (1983) contends, helps to reveal nonobvious features of our experienced world. Through interaction, replay, and so forth, the computer affords the user many opportunities for reflecting on his or her actions.

Older subjects performed better on the computer versions of the imagery tasks. This finding was not unexpected; the images used in the computer version were analogs of the actual objects in the video version and thus more abstract. At the same time, this abstract quality is an asset for the two transformational tasks, which require the subject to coordinate changes in two dimensions. The critical information, such as the angle of the cheerleader's legs or the arc of the clothesline, is highlighted, and distractions, such as background, are minimized. While the taped sequences used for the video tasks were quite realistic, the actual transformation that formed the basis for the problem may have been difficult to separate from the background. In the computer task, each object was clear and distinct. In the video task, the scene within which the task was embedded may have been too saturated with extraneous information. Although the computer tasks had the same major referent points, the objects had a crisper appearance than they did in the background scene shot for video. Each object was clearly outlined and depicted in brightly contrasting colors. The video sequence is more muted in over-all appearance.

The computer task more closely approximates the computer and video games that are popular among children and young adults. Many of these individuals are used to working with fast-moving animation, and they are familiar with analogic characters. All subjects were asked about their previous experience with computers, computer and video games, video recorders, and so forth. The most common experience was with computer and video games, and many children had video game systems in their homes. It should also be noted that experience with computers was varied, ranging from those who had no experience at all to those who were attending a computer camp at the time of the research. The type and level of experience had no effect on performance of the task. One interesting sidelight came from a question posed to subjects about their preference for using computers or videotape to solve problems. Older subjects (middle school, high school, and college) preferred videotape, although their performance was better on the computer. In contrast, younger subjects preferred the computer, a preference that was not clearly reflected in their performance.

This study supports the notion that computer and video versions of the same task require different performance strategies. The computer tasks involved the use of symbols that were more abstract than the representations used with the video tasks. Complex problems involving transformations are presented in a clear and concise manner on the computer. In general, performance was more accurate for the computer versions of tasks, which suggests that the unique presentation techniques and interactive qualities of the computer are ideal for presenting tasks involving imagery.

Conclusions

The computer is an exciting tool for the study of children's spatial cognition, and it may have potential for enhancing children's experiences with the spatial and visual world. Developmental researchers need to consider the computer as an important methodological tool that can assist them in the study of spatial thought and imagery. Clearly, no definite conclusions can be reached as to whether the computer actually influences the development of spatial or imaginal skills in more than a heuristic fashion. However, Bamberger (1983, p. 34) suggests that the computer can highlight important knowledge: "The computer world can, as a hall of mirrors, reflect [this] commonsense knowledge back to us in a new guise. Playing with what we make in the computer world — 'generating' it — we can come to see familiar objects and actions in new ways, and we can come to a new appreciation of the intuitions with which we make the things we know best." More research is needed, both descriptive and experimental, into children's interactions with computers in a wide variety of contexts. As this research is done, we may discover that the computer helps to open up new views of self and the world.

References

Acker, S., and Klein, E. "Visualizing Spatial Tasks: A Comparison of Computer Graphic and Full-Band Video Displays." *Educational Communications and Technology Journal,* in press.

Baggett, P. "Structurally Equivalent Stories in Movies and Text and the Effect of Medium on Recall." *Journal of Verbal Learning and Verbal Behavior,* 1979, *18,* 333–356.

Balanchine, G. "Preface." In A. Hutchinson, *Labanotation: A System of Analyzing and Recording Movement.* New York: Theatre Arts Books, 1970.

Bamberger, J. "The Computer as Sand Castle." In *Chameleon in the Classroom: Developing Roles for Computers.* Technical Report No. 22. New York: Bank Street College of Education, 1983.

Bork, A. "Learning with Computer Simulation." *Computer.* October 1979, pp. 75–84.

Cambre, M. *The Effects of Message Design Variables on the Appeal and Comprehension of Computer-Generated Instructional Animation.* Final Report, Spencer Foundation Grants to Young Scholars. Columbus: The Ohio State University, 1983.

Char, C., and Meringoff, L. *The Role of Story Illustrations: Children's Story Comprehensions in Three Different Media.* Technical Report No. 22, Harvard Project Zero. Cambridge, Mass.: Harvard University, 1981.

Chatman, S. "What a Novel Can Do That Films Can't (and Vice Versa)." *Critical Inquiry,* 1980, *7,* 121–140.

Csuri, C. "Computer Graphics and Art." *IEEE Proceedings,* 1974, *62* (4), 503–515.

Csuri, C. "3-D Computer Animation." In M. Robinoff and M. Youitts (Eds.), *Advances in Computers.* Vol. 16. New York: Academic Press, 1977.

Dean, A. "The Structure of Imagery." *Child Development,* 1976, *47,* 949–958.

diSessa, A. "Unlearning Aristotelian Physics: A Study of Knowledge-Based Learning." *Cognitive Science,* 1982, *6,* 37–75.

Glick, J. "Discussion." In *Chameleon in the Classroom: Developing Roles for Computers.* Technical Report No. 22. New York: Bank Street College of Education, 1983.

Greenfield, P. *Mind and Media: The Effects of Television, Video Games, and Computers.* Cambridge, Mass.: Harvard University Press, 1984.

Hammond, K. "Computer Graphics as an Aid to Learning." *Science,* 1971, *173,* 903–907.

Hooper, K. "The Use of Computer Graphics in the Development of Mathematical Imagery." Paper presented at the annual meeting of the American Educational Research Association, New York, 1982.

Hortin, J. "Introspection and Visual Thinking for the Instructional Technologist." *Educational Technology,* 1982, *22* (6), 23–24.

Hughes, W. "A Study of the Use of Computer-Simulated Experiments in the Physics Classroom." *Journal of Computer-Based Instruction,* 1974, *1,* 1–6.

Klein, E., and Acker, S. "Anticipatory Imagery Tasks Presented as Video and Computer Graphic Stories: Exploring Media Differences in Symbolic Form." Paper presented at the 14th Annual Symposium of the Jean Piaget Society, Philadelphia, 1984.

Klein, E., and Liben, L. "Mental Imagery and Operativity: Children's Use of Static, Kinetic, and Transformational Imagery." Paper presented at the 11th Annual Symposium of the Jean Piaget Society, Philadelphia, 1981.

Kosslyn, S. *Image and Mind.* Cambridge, Mass.: Harvard University Press, 1980.

Liben, L. "Spatial Representation and Behavior: Multiple Perspectives." In L. Liben, A. Patterson, and N. Newcombe (Eds.), *Spatial Representation and Behavior Across the Life Span.* New York: Academic Press, 1981.

Lowery, B., and Knirk, F. "Microcomputer Video Games and Spatial Visualization Acquisition." *Journal of Educational Technology Systems,* 1982–1983, *11* (2), 155–166.

Malone, T. *What Makes Things Fun to Learn? A Study of Intrinsically Motivating Computer Games.* Cognitive and Instructional Science Series CIS-7 (SSL-80-11). Palo Alto, Calif.: Xerox Research Center, 1980.

Malone, T. "Toward a Theory of Intrinsically Motivating Instruction." *Cognitive Science,* 1981, *5,* 333–370.

Meringoff, L., Vibbert, M., Char, C., Fernie, D., Barker, C., and Gardner, H. "How Is Children's Learning from Television Distinctive? Exploiting the Medium Methodologically." In J. Bryant and D. Anderson (Eds.), *Children's Understanding of Television.* New York: Academic Press, 1983.

Olson, D., and Bruner, J. "Learning Through Experience and Learning Through Media." In D. Olson (Ed.), *Media and Symbols: The Forms of Expression, Communication, and Education.* 73rd Yearbook of the National Society for the Study of Education. Chicago: University of Chicago Press, 1974.

Papert, S. *Mindstorms: Children, Computers, and Powerful Ideas.* New York: Basic Books, 1980.

Piaget, J. "The Role of Action in the Development of Thinking." In W. Overton and J. Gallagher (Eds.), *Knowledge and Development.* Vol. 1. New York: Plenum Press, 1977.

Piaget, J., and Inhelder, B. *Mental Imagery in the Child.* New York: Basic Books, 1971.

Piaget, J., and Inhelder, B. *Memory and Intelligence.* New York: Basic Books, 1973.

Pleck, M. "On the Role of Computer Graphics in Engineering Design Graphics Course." Paper presented at the annual meeting of the American Society for Engineering Education, 1975. (ED 116 954)

Salomon, G. "What Is Learned and How It Is Taught: The Interaction Between Media, Message, Task, and Learner." In D. Olson (Ed.), *Media and Symbols: The Forms of Expression, Communication, and Education.* Chicago: University of Chicago Press, 1974.

Salomon, G. "Shape, Not Only Content: How Media Symbols Partake in the Development of Abilities." In E. Wartella (Ed.), *Children Communicating: Media and Development of Thought, Speech, Understanding.* Beverly Hills, Calif.: Sage, 1979.

Savage, G., and Officer, J. "CHOREO: An Interactive Computer Model for Dance." *International Journal of Man-Machine Studies,* May 1978.

Shepard, R., and Metzler, J. "Mental Rotation of Three-Dimensional Objects." *Science,* 1971, *191,* 952–954.

Wegman, E. "Computer Graphics in Undergraduate Statistics." *International Journal of Mathematical Education in Science and Technology,* 1974, *5* (1), 15–23.

Wozny, M. "Interactive Computer Graphics for Engineering Education." *Professional Engineer,* 1978, *48* (6), 14–18.

*Elisa L. Klein is assistant professor of education at
The Ohio State University. Her research interests concern
cognitive development in children, including the development
of mental imagery, and the role of computers in development
and learning.*

This chapter discusses some of the philosophical and empirical implications for developmental psychology of the prospect of human-computer intelligent systems, which can work together to solve problems, learn, and develop.

Integrating Human and Computer Intelligence

Roy D. Pea

The thesis to be explored in this chapter is that advances in computer applications and artificial intelligence have important implications for the study of development and learning in psychology. I begin by reviewing current approaches to the use of computers as devices for solving problems, reasoning, and thinking. I then raise questions concerning the integration of computer-based intelligence with human intelligence to serve human development and the processes of education.

Expert Systems and Intelligent Tutoring Systems

Until recently, written texts have been the principal means for storing the knowledge needed to solve complex problems. Computers have provided a radically new medium for storing and making use of expert knowledge. Expert systems are programs that embody the knowledge of experts in making judgments in a field. Such systems emulate the reasoning and problem-solving abilities of human experts, and they are widely used as advisory aids in human decision making. They vary greatly in their representations of knowledge, its accessibility, its ease of modification, and in the degree to which it attempts to

E. L. Klein (Ed.). *Children and Computers.* New Directions for
Child Development, no. 28. San Francisco: Jossey-Bass, June 1985.

teach its user. Today, dozens of such systems serve as powerful conceptual tools for the extension and redefinition of human intellectual efforts in science, medicine, industry, programming, and education. Excellent accounts of existing expert systems and their growing importance are provided in Feigenbaum and McCorduck (1983). Prominent examples include MYCIN (Shortliffe, 1976), a medical expert system; MOLGEN (Friedland, 1979), an expert system used to design experiments in molecular genetics; and DENDRAL (Lindsay and others, 1980), an expert chemistry system used in determining the molecular structure of unknown organic compounds. Expert systems are also used as aids in ill-defined creative tasks, such as the design of integrated circuits (Stefik and de Kleer, 1983).

The heart of the process of transferring expertise to the machine lies in reducing experts' know-how to chunks of knowledge specified, for example, in terms of productions of if-then rules; that is, if specific conditions are present in a situation, then a certain action is taken (Davis and Lenat, 1981; Hayes-Roth and others, 1984). Methods for mining experts' knowledge are related to both the clinical interviewing techniques familiar to developmentalists and the think-aloud protocol methods common to cognitive psychology. The aim is to work with the experts to help them articulate what they know. Then, the domain-specific facts, algorithms, heuristics, general problem-solving strategies, and systematic understanding of a domain (for example, causal laws, probabilities) that the experts have available can be codified in computer programs that mimic the solution of novel real-world problems at an expert level of performance. The system comes to emulate human expertise through recursive iterations that eliminate the differences between experts' judgments and those of the expert system.

The problem of transfer of expertise (Barr and others, 1979) raises a host of developmental concerns: "For an expert system to be truly useful, it should be able to learn what human experts know, so that it can perform as well as they do, understand the points of departure among the views of human experts who disagree, keep its knowledge up to date as human experts do (by reading, asking questions, and learning from experience), and present its reasoning to its human users in much the way that human experts would (justifying, clarifying, explaining, and even tutoring)" (Barr and Feigenbaum, 1982, p. 80). This passage implies that system users and knowledge sources (the "experts") are in relevant respects homogeneous in knowledge. However, the knowledge in an expert system and its power are not immediately accessible to a novice, much less to a child. Most expert systems act as advisers for consultation on specific problems. They can rarely solve problems autonomously. Thus, many techniques need to be learned in order to make effective use of expert systems.

Creating systems that children can use constitutes an important problem for education and developmental psychology. The developmentalist asks the reverse of the knowledge engineer's question: How can the expertise transferred from human adults to computers be transferred back by computer to the child? The adult version (how can novices effectively use and understand the problem-solving activities of an expert system?) is now being addressed in the design of intelligent expert systems. Intelligent expert systems give correct answers or useful advice in problem situations. They also use concepts and reasoning processes that resemble those that the system user might employ. A major problem in engineering such systems has been in creating facilities that can give an explanatory account, in terms that one expects from a human, of the reasoning that underlies the advice offered.

What is the potential for expert systems for human learning and development? Can expert systems eventually offer students better access to knowledge and opportunities for development than either most teachers or spontaneous experience alone can provide? We come closer to answering these questions by considering intelligent tutoring systems — systems that go beyond possessing expert knowledge and attempt to model the student's knowledge and the learning process for acquiring expertise. These intelligent tutoring systems are designed to support students in gaining access to the expert system. For example, SOPHIE (Brown and others, 1982) functions both as an expert system and as a teaching system in prompting the student to form and test hypotheses about an electronic power supply circuit. SOPHIE has two different modes: One poses troubleshooting problems for a single person; the other simulates a gaming situation in which one team sets a fault for another team to diagnose. In the solo mode, the system sets a fault for the student to diagnose in a power supply circuit. The student can measure voltages and currents in different parts of the circuit by asking questions of the system; the aim is to figure out which component is faulty. The system evaluates the student's hypotheses about the fault by analyzing what it has told the student up to that point about the values in different components of the system and by comparing these values with the values that would obtain under the student's hypotheses. This kind of comparison involves very sophisticated circuit simulation and fault propagation techniques. The same capabilities are used to tutor students in the team gaming option. Other systems that attempt to understand the user are DEBUGGY (Burton, 1982) and ACM (Langley and others, 1984), which diagnose students' procedural errors in base-ten subtraction; the WHY system (Stevens and others, 1979), which teaches the geographical aspects of rainfall distribution by initiating a Socratic dialogue; and Boyle and Anderson's (1984) system for teaching proof procedures in high school geometry, which explicitly tutors problem-solving strategies for the construction of geometric proofs. These systems vary in the degree to which their cognitive diagnostics are theoretically and empirically substantiated.

From a developmental perspective, the educational use of expert systems must be concerned with how the novice can be supported in learning from and making use of this form of knowledge storage. Certain types of expert systems have exciting educational potential. The design of such systems must be guided by the need to address students' lack of knowledge about either the expert domain or the methods for operating the systems that use such information storage. An important task remains in creating systems capable of providing interactive environments that succeed in integrating students' intuitive theories of domain knowledge constructed through everyday experience, such as in physics (diSessa, 1983), with formal domain knowledge. Research is needed on how children's use of such systems affects the relation between cognitive development and learning. For example, how does the child novice differ from the adult novice for particular content domains, such as geometry? In the context of this question, such computer-based systems appear to have theoretical import for developmental psychology, in ways now to be addressed.

Changes in Views on Cognitive Development

After describing some characterizations of cognitive development as the construction of an invariantly ordered sequence of universal stages, I will review some recent challenges to these universal descriptions. These considerations will lead to an examination of potential uses of computer expert systems and intelligent tutoring systems for the reconceptualizing of cognitive development and to more drastic reformulations of the agenda for developmental studies.

Constructivism and Stages in Developmental Psychology. In recent decades, developmental psychologists have been preoccupied with the ongoing debate concerning research into stages of cognitive development. Driven by the seminal studies of Piaget (1983), developmental psychologists throughout the world have sought to substantiate and finely delineate the broad universal stages of cognitive development that Piaget proposed.

Piaget defined four broad stages of intellectual or cognitive development: the sensorimotor, the preoperational, the concrete operational, and the formal operational. Although recent formulations (Case, 1985; Fischer, 1980) differ in emphasis, they maintain a roughly comparable picture. Stages are major qualitative breaks in cognitive functioning that, according to Piaget (1973) have four characteristics: First, they are ordered in sequence. Second, they are integrative, in that earlier stages are an integral part of later stages. Third, they are characterized by a "whole structure," which in the case of intelligence means by an underlying system of logical operations. Fourth, in any series of stages, there is a distinction between the process of formation and the final forms of equilibrium; that is, they are progressively constructed without total preformation.

In describing the formation of the stages, Piaget placed central emphasis on constructivism, the perspective that emphasizes the interaction of the endogenous character of the organism and environment in the organism's construction of progressively more advanced stages of knowledge. Piaget (1973, pp. 2–3) emphatically contrasted the "spontaneous" or subject-initiated discovery, learning, and inventing that contribute to the construction of these broad systems of operations with "other" learning, such as the learning that occurs in schools. "I have in mind only the *truly* psychological development of the child as opposed to his school development or to his family development; that is, I will above all stress the spontaneous aspect of this development, though I will limit myself to the purely intellectual and cognitive development. Actually we can distinguish two aspects in the child's intellectual development. On the one hand, we have what may be called the psychosocial aspect, that is, everything the child receives from without and learns in general by family, school, educative transmission. On the other there is the development which can be called spontaneous. For the sake of abbreviation I will call it psychological, the development of the intelligence itself — what the child learns by himself, what none can teach him and he must discover alone; and it is essentially this development which takes time . . . it is precisely this spontaneous development which forms the obvious and necessary condition for the school development." As I will later suggest, symbolic activities with the computer may necessitate a reformulation of the concept of spontaneous learning, since the world of physical objects for child play and action is remarkably expandable through programmable symbols.

Challenges to the Piagetian Enterprise. There have been several areas of research that converge as problematic for Piaget's conceptions of development. I will review three fundamental areas: findings on the role of sociocultural factors in learning and development, on giftedness and prodigies, and on the role of knowledge in computer expert systems.

Piaget has been extensively criticized for underplaying the contribution of sociocultural factors to development (Rogoff and Lave, 1984). Contemporary work has been influenced by the theories of the Soviet psychologist L. S. Vygotsky (Rogoff and Wertsch, 1984; Laboratory of Comparative Human Cognition, 1983), who saw sociocultural factors as having important consequences on higher-level cognitive development. Formal operations are nonuniversal, particularly in cultures without schooling, a finding that was troubling even for Piaget (1972). What Piaget described as spontaneous learning is apparently insufficient to enable humans to think in terms of operations on operations, the definition of formal thought. Educational processes of sociocultural transmission, especially those involving abstract symbolic systems, such as logic, mathematics, and written language, play an essential role in the formation of such thought patterns (Laboratory of Comparative Human Cognition, 1983; Olson and Bruner, 1974).

Research inspired by Vygotsky has great significance for computer-based extensions and redefinitions of human intelligence. Vygotsky's (1978) dynamic conception of the "zone of proximal development" concerns phases in ontogenesis in which a child has partly mastered a skill but can act more effectively with the assistance of a more skilled peer or adult. The zone of proximal development is the region of skill effectiveness that lies between the child's independent functioning and the child's functioning with social support. Intelligence is viewed as a collective activity jointly accomplished between child and more able others before the child can function intelligently on his or her own. In contrast to Piaget, Vygotsky (quoted by Rogoff and Wertsch, 1984, p. 3), argued that "instruction is only good when it proceeds ahead of development. It then awakens and rouses to life those functions which are in a stage of maturing, which lie in the zone of proximal development. It is in this way that instruction plays an extremely important role in development." The central implication is that the problem-solving system formed by child and more competent others — broadened here to include computer systems — is an especially appropriate unit of analysis for studies of the development of problem-solving skills.

Findings on Giftedness and Prodigies. Further evidence against the universalist architecture of Piagetian theory is found in cognitive studies with children identified as gifted or as prodigious in their performances in such domains as mathematics, music, chess, or composition. Research on giftedness and prodigy performances among children (Feldman, 1980; 1982; Gardner, 1983) demonstrates that such individuals are not in an advanced Piagetian stage of development across tasks but that they perform on Piaget-based measures much like their same-age cohorts, even as they outperform most adults in their forte. Prior attainment of the general logical structures defining the Piagetian formal operational period is not, as these exceptional individuals illustrate, necessary for high-level domain-specific intellectual performances.

According to Gardner (1983, p. 27), a pluralistic approach to cognition, which focuses on the domain specificity of intellectual performances rather than on transdomain universal stages, posits that, "irrespective of domains, there should (in proper Piagetian fashion) be a stagelike sequence through which any individual must pass. However, individuals differ greatly from one another in the speed with which they pass through these domains; and, contra Piaget, success at negotiating one domain entails no necessary correlation with speed or success in negotiating other domains. . . . Moreover, progress in a domain does not depend entirely on the solitary individual's actions within his world. Rather, much of the information about the domain is better thought of as contained within the culture itself, for it is the culture that defines the stages and fixes the limits of individual achievement. One must conceive of the individual *and* his culture as embodying a certain stage sequence, with much of the information essential for development inhering in the culture itself rather than simply inside the individual's skull." This perspective on the development of intelligence has provocative implications for marrying the problem-solving capabilities of child and computer. Since there are distinct developmental trajectories for different content domains, rather than a general logical engine on which the development of cognitive skills in specific domains depends, then integrations are in principle possible between childhood thinking and expert or intelligent tutoring computer systems that provide developmental technologies. These integrations would serve as mental catalysts for engineering the development of high-level cognitive skills. The child would not need to await the development of general logical structures in order to become a powerful thinker.

The Role of Knowledge in Expert Systems. Similar arguments are provided by research on artificial intelligence (AI) systems. Cognitive scientists have found that extensive knowledge is necessary for expert-level performance in solving problems in every content area studied. Waldrop (1984, p. 1279) reached the conclusion that "the essence of intelligence seems to be less a matter of reasoning ability than of knowing a lot about the world." This presents a clear problem for the Piagetian approach, in which the underlying logical schemes involved in the reasoning behind a task are considered to be the core of intellectual functioning. The principal mechanisms distinguishing what Piaget described as the stages of intelligence are, for example, defined in terms of the logical operations of reasoning characteristic of that stage. What is the role for knowledge? Here Piaget introduced the convenient abstraction of *decalage* in order to deal with the theoretically inconvenient differences in the average age at which, for example, the concept of conservation is acquired for the different materials of weight, volume, and number (different content domains). The role of specific knowledge is accorded a minor role.

What are we to do, then, with knowledge in an age in which intelligent behavior is being modeled by computers and in which reasoning mechanisms, although necessary, are far less important than the web of propositions and rules that define knowledge and cognitive skill? If the weak end of the machinery of cognitive development lies in building up the appropriately organized store of knowledge structures (Carey, 1984), how then can knowledge be better acquired? How can computers as intelligent tutoring systems and learning machines in their own right help the student to develop such knowledge?

Although in broad outline the interactionist perspective that Piaget offers may be correct, the three groups of studies just reviewed imply a different vision of what constitutes the interaction environment basic to learning and development and of what experiences warrant the description of spontaneous learning through solitary discovery. The culture, as expressed through more knowledgeable others, provides apprenticeship models for the development of cognitive skills and offers advice and hints to help structure the child's discovery space as he or she proceeds through the zones of proximal development. Left to her or his own spontaneous discoveries, the child as intuitive scientist arrives too often at theories of how the physical or mathematical world works that are at odds with appropriate formal theories (A. L. Brown, 1984; Gentner and Stevens, 1983). We find eroding the artificial distinction between what one discovers alone (what Piaget chauvinistically describes as true development) and what one discovers with the aid of others, however indirect that aid may be. Children need not — indeed, in most instances, they will not — reinvent through spontaneous discovery the conceptually adequate theories about the world that science has taken centuries to identify and formulate.

Developmental Theory and Human-Computer Systems

In this section, I will consider some major questions that the possibility of human-computer intelligent systems raises for developmental theory and some of the rich prospects they offer for psychological research and for the promotion of education and development.

Two possibly but not necessarily interconnected roles for the creation of such systems may be distinguished. The first is as research tool for developmental and cognitive psychology; the second is as educational tool. In terms of the first role, by configuring the system in different ways, different explanatory models of learning and development can directly be tested. These models might be concerned with one or another of several issues: assessing whether systems that give the student prompts to promote self-questioning, planning, and monitoring lead to more effective metacognition and learning to learn (J. S. Brown, 1984; Palinscar and Brown, 1984); ascertaining the kinds of prodevelopmental roles of conflict or of confrontation of "bugs" in student understanding in developmental reorganizations of knowledge systems (Siegler, 1983); testing our understanding of the heuristics that expert teachers use to model a student's understanding and providing new learning experiences and environments at the appropriate level (Collins and Stevens, 1982; Sleeman and Brown, 1982); and providing testing grounds for knowledge assessment and cognitive diagnostics and explicit tests of intervention hypotheses in training studies (Boyle and Anderson, 1984). In terms of the second role, for educational purposes, systems can be constructed to be used autonomously by students as tools for learning new fields of knowledge and for acquiring problem-solving and problem-defining skills for specific domains.

In the paragraphs that follow, major challenges to developmental psychology posed by the coupling of human and computer intelligence are roughly ordered from the conservative to the radical in their implications. At the conservative end, they merely carry forward modifications to the Piagetian enterprise; at the radical extreme, they portend the coevolution of human and computer intelligence.

Computers and the Zone of Proximal Development. It is possible that future versions of AI systems could serve as tools for helping children move through the zones of proximal development by extending the "social" environment for cognitive growth by interactively providing hints and support in problem-solving tasks like the ones adults provide. Computers playing this role will be the information age sequel to concepts of a zone of proximal development (ZPD), in which the adult human plays the tutorial role of coconstructing with the child his or her latent developmental capabilities. In this case, the zone of proximal development is traversed with the complementary capabilities of the human-computer system. However, unlike those who have conducted most ZPD studies, I do not assume that self-sufficiency is the telos of such learning activities. Many forms of cognitive activity may require the continuing intervention of an intelligent computer system, for effectiveness or because of their complexity. Similarly, not all cognitive tasks for which ZPDs can be arranged should be ones that the child is expected to internalize for subsequent solo performances. Solo performances are not realistic in terms of the ways in which intelligent activities are organized and accomplished in the real world. They are often collaborative, depend on resources beyond an individual's long-term memory, and require the use of information-handling tools. If we took away from practicing thinkers and practitioners what we take away from children to assess their cognitive functioning, scientists could not do science, mathematicians could not do math, historians could not do history, and policy makers could not make policy. The level of task understanding necessary for the child alone is an empirical question that remains to be answered, domain by domain. For example, in arithmetical understanding, educators now emphasize estimation skills over calculation skills as the use of calculators has become widespread.

In terms of computer-based ZPD tools, there are two major ways of transforming the zone of learning environments in which interactions toward development emerge. First, microworlds, which are fairly conservative in their implications, can be created for the promotion of domain expertise; second, there are cognitive trace systems, which are more radical in their potential powers.

Microworld Pedagogic Systems. Pedagogic systems focus on cognitive self-sufficiency, much like existing educational programs, in contrast to pragmatic systems, which allow for precocious intellectual performances of which the child may be incapable without the system's support. We thus need to distinguish between systems in which the child uses tools provided by the computer system to solve problems that he or she cannot solve alone and systems in which the system establishes that the child understands the problem-solving processes thereby achieved. We can call the first kind of system pragmatic and the second pedagogic. Pragmatic systems may have the peripheral consequence of pedagogical effects, that is, they may contribute to understanding but not necessarily. The aim of pedagogic systems is to facilitate, through interaction, the development of the human intelligent system. While there is a grey area in between, and some systems may serve both functions, clear cases of each can be defined.

Pedagogic systems that use microworld provide rich opportunities for development and learning. A microworld is a structured environment that allows the learner to explore and manipulate a rule-governed universe, subject to specific assumptions and constraints, that serves as an analogical representation of some aspects of the natural world. Microworlds have other properties that cannot be described here (Papert, 1980). Pedagogic systems can use microworlds to further redefine the objects of the spontaneous learning that Piaget considered integral to development when he argued that each time one prematurely teaches a child something he could have discovered for himself, the child is kept from inventing it and consequently understanding it completely (Piaget, 1983). But, discovery by oneself is not well defined, and interactive software can further blur the distinction. Computer objects could be programmed so that the child would be subtly guided to discover them. They could provide discovery situations that conflict with the inferred worldview of the child because they are "smart" with knowledge of the flawed theories that children construct en route to expertise. For such pedagogic systems to work in promoting learning and development, we need research on the prodevelopmental roles of conflict or disequilibrium and a theory of how and when hints toward discovery are successful (Sleeman and Brown, 1982).

Microworld pedagogic systems could provide environments enabling students to learn skills and knowledge in specific domains by observing modeling of the process of solving example problems, by doing, by discovery, and by instruction. An aim can be to replicate the coincidences (Feldman, 1980, 1982) of factors that appear to lead to prodigious cognitive performances. This involves providing suitable models, a learning environment with cognitively appropriate help facilities that embody cultural knowledge and that is sufficiently engaging to command the child's intensive efforts.

Pedagogic Cognitive Trace Systems. Pedagogic systems could also be created that transform what will happen in the learning environment in ways that cannot be anticipated without building prototypes and doing observations. Cognitive trace systems can provide a major lever for cognitive development by providing tools for reflection. The fundamental idea of a cognitive trace system is that the intermediate products of mind are externalized through the process of interacting with knowledge-based computer systems. These traces expand the cognitive workspace to include a trail, as it were, of where one has been in an episode of problem solving. Thus, remembering where one has been does not interfere with ongoing processes of creation or problem solving. Such traces would provide richer sources for assessing the student's knowledge than any teacher only observing student behaviors without the system could ever process and use for effective instruction.

Cognitive trace systems may have dramatic consequences for how human beings develop cognitive skills. These systems are instances of the thinking tools provided by other symbolic media — writing, mathematics, logic, and programming — that render human thought processes external for inspection, analysis, and reflection and that have forever transformed our world of thought and action (Ong, 1982).

Three major functions can be imagined for such traces. First, for the child, an examination of these cognitive traces, possibly prompted by the computer at appropriate junctures of thought, could lead to an emergent awareness of errors in understanding. In some cases, this could also lead to an understanding of errors of execution, which misdirect the search for solution. Second, for the psychologist or teacher, such traces could be used to diagnose a child's understandings and potentially bug-ridden ideas of the domain under study and to identify the learning experiences that are necessary for instructional remediation. Third, for the computer, such traces could be used to build a model of the child's understanding and then provide next-step responsive environments.

A prototype of such a cognitive trace system has been built by John Seeley Brown and colleagues at the Xerox Palo Alto Research Center (J. S. Brown, 1984). In this system, called AlgebraLand, the computer carries out low-level procedures for transforming equations while students focus on their strategies for choosing the procedures that the computer will perform on equations. The cognitive trace function is expressed in an updated topological graph of the student's problem-solving steps. With this trace path, the student can "read" the alternative solution paths that she or he tried in order to learn from experience why some were successful and others less so.

As Boden (1979) notes in discussing Piaget's work on the development of purposive self-knowledge, children can or try to do many tasks without knowing how they do so, often without being able to correct their failures. She discusses Piaget's (1976, p. 340) account of how consciousness moves from periphery to center, since deliberate action first involves awareness only of the goal and of whether success or failure occurs, "while the fact that the scheme that assigns a goal to the action immediately triggers off the means of affecting it may remain unconscious." Later, largely because of the child's search for the reasons underlying his or her errors, consciousness "moves in the direction of the central regions of the action in order to reach its internal mechanism: recognition of the means employed, reasons for their selection or their modification en route, and the like." Cognitive trace systems could act as prime movers toward the child's grasp of consciousness in different domains by contributing to the development of this metacognitive knowledge, so important for expertise (Brown and others, 1983). But, we first will need research to determine whether such cognitive trace facilities do indeed make developmental contributions.

Integrating Child and Computer Information-Processing Systems. It is now commonplace to note limitations in human symbol manipulation abilities. As Siegler (1983, p. 129–130) observes, many "processing limitations can prevent people from attaining their goals: limitations on the number of symbols that they can manipulate simultaneously, on the speed with which they can manipulate symbols, on the depth to which they can search memory, and on their resistance to interference, to name but four." It has become a central goal of cognitive and developmental psychology in recent years to document how we utilize strategies to overcome these processing limitations of short-term memory (through such mnemonic strategies as rehearsal, elaboration, and organization) and long-term memory (through books and other materials).

Integrating the powerful information-processing systems of the computer and the frail information-processing system of the human mind may be possible. If such integration is successful, it may have great consequence for cognitive development. Empirical studies during the past decade have extensively demonstrated young children's preconcious understanding of such complex concepts as causality, number, conservation, proportions, and logical deduction in simplified task environments that avoid taxing the limits of their information-processing systems (for reviews, see Carey, 1984; Case, 1984; Donaldson, 1978). Yet it is still conventional wisdom that student access to many disciplines, such as statistics, must await a certain age. In principle, we may be able to close much of the gap between the information-processing capabilities of child and adult and ultimately of humans and computers by integrating our information-processing systems.

One central hope is that such integrated systems may provide a path out of the breakdowns of rational thinking that have been extensively catalogued recently and that appear to result in large part from the bottlenecks of human information processing. The work of Kahnemann and others (1982) on judgment under uncertainty, of Wason and Johnson-Laird (1972) on the attentional bias to positive evidence in deductive reasoning, of Luria (1976) and of Scribner (1977) on the empirical bias in logical reasoning, of Shweder (1980) and others on statistical thinking, and of Nisbett and Ross (1980) on errors in social judgment has revealed the widespread use of heuristics for thinking that leads to erroneous conclusions. We have already noted the non-universality of formal operational thinking, particularly in cultures without schooling. There should be more effective ways for people to develop these problem-solving powers. Too many people have trouble learning the formal rule- and model-oriented disciplines that pervade the modern information age — ranging from physics and mathematics to the genetic code in biology and computer programming — and the kind of problem-solving skills required for job and life successes. We are also so prone to errors of judgment, errors of reasoning, and lack of monitoring and evaluation in our decision making that most of us most of the time could usefully be propped up and reminded to become more effective.

Could AI systems be used to buttress these well-known human frailities? Could they serve educational processes of cultural transmission and redefinition in a computer age? With the integration of human and computer intelligent systems, we may be able to attenuate human processing limitations. One possible way of dealing with the problem posed by the cognitive interface between software and the child's mind is to work at providing the set of computational tools necessary so that intermediary cognitive work, which usually goes on in the child's mind and strains age-related memory and processing limitations, can become virtually perceptual work, unrestricted by such limits. The store and processes of the mind needed for problem solving can be those of the child-computer system rather than of the child only. The cognitive workspace could be expanded to include the computer screen and other computational devices.

With such systems, we may thus extend the forms of thought made possible by the symbols that Vygotsky (1978) describes as "external memory aids" to the mind — mathematics, written language, logic, and programming languages. For any content domain, from Siegler's (1983) balance beams to correlations, we should be able to build devices that enable children to circumvent the processing limitations that hamper their ability to engage in higher forms of reasoning and thinking, such as concrete and formal operational thinking. The principal caveat is that we have to show how such adjuncts to processing capacity can be designed and developed for specific knowledge domains. Only then will we find the practical obstacles to their effective use in childhood education.

Pragmatic Cognitive Tools for Higher-Level Achievements. To go further, one can imagine the invention of powerful cognitive tools that would support problem solving in domains previously considered to be difficult or even impossible for young children. In other words, programs could be devised that would serve as "cognitive props" for complex problem solving. For example, by using these programs children who were not formal operational thinkers would solve abstract problems that require formal operations.

Dennett (1978) argues that when a system, such as a software system, gets sufficiently complicated, we change the focus of descriptions from physical to intentional properties. As observers, we adopt the intentional stance and describe the system as thinking, believing, and with other intentional terms. The same is true when we discuss human-computer systems. We adopt the expert stance by attributing to such systems expertise and intelligence that we normally reserve for the human adult. We say that the system is formal operational, or clever, or very good at solving algebra problems rather than focus on the individual as the unit of developmental analysis. In fact, we can extend the well-known Turing test, a thought experiment proposed by Alan Turing (1950), to the idea of human-computer intelligent systems. In this test, a blind evaluation question-and-answer format is used to determine whether an object possesses thought. However, the Turing test is nondevelopmental; that is, it does not distinguish qualitatively different levels of intelligence. Given a developmental revision, such a test might be used to evaluate behaviors of an integrated human-computer intelligence system. Consider a child who approaches a formal operational task. The child alone may not be formal operational in his or her thinking. However, working with the computer system, the child may indeed be able to successfully solve formal operational cognitive tasks (such as control of variables or proportional reasoning). The integrated child-computer system is evaluated by the Turing test as formal operational.

This argument rests on the genetic epistemology of symbol systems. What are the implications of a tool of human intelligence for cultural development? Just as other symbol systems, such as mathematics, logic, and written language, have transformed our intellectual powers, so in principle can intelligent computer systems transform them. The concept of intelligent human-computer systems is simply an extension of this generally recognized developmental empowering by symbol systems. What makes the computer unique is its potential for modeling human intelligence. As thinking tools, computers have considerably greater potential than tools of the past, because effective use of such intellectual tools as mathematics and written language is constrained by our limited memory and information-processing abilities

(Minsky, 1983; Simon, 1977). We now have extensive gaps between competence and performance in cognitive functioning, but these gaps may narrow when human and computer intelligence are married.

This argument contrasts with Piaget's contention that better teaching and earlier experiences of the right kind cannot lead to precocious intellectual performances. He responds to the so-called American question (of accelerated instruction) by criticizing Bruner's (1960) claim that any idea, problem, or body of knowledge can be presented in a form simple enough that any particular learner can understand it. Piaget (1971, p. 21) argues that "intellectual growth contains its own rhythm. Speeding up cannot be indefinitely continued." Piaget's argument is essentially that education can at best accelerate stage development within certain limits. Successive reorganizations of knowledge exemplified by the stages are time-consuming and take much experience.

But we may resurrect these questions, since the potential of AI systems may change the terms of the acceleration debate. One may agree with Piaget's notions about the structural limitations to educational acceleration. However, Piaget's reservations were based on the performances of a solitary child. Yet children's problem-solving skills may be stretched beyond their potential when they receive aid from others, such as peers and adults. Performance in what Vygotsky called the zone of proximal development has important implications for intelligent tutoring systems that can in principle be extended to human-computer intelligent systems. It has even more radical implications for Piaget's objections to the American question.

The radical implications center on the capabilities of young children when supported by intelligent computer systems. Some developmentalists have been dissatisfied with the ZPD studies because they also view the solitary performance of the child as the fundamental unit for developmental analysis (seeing additional aids, coaching, and prompting by an adult as "cheating" in this respect), yet the issue becomes more controversial when the child is part of a human-computer intelligent system. Imagine a typical nine-year-old working with an expert system to solve formal operational problems on correlations that involve multiple variables. The child-computer system solves the problem through the integration of the computer and the child's currently functioning solitary intelligence. As already noted, the system would be considered formal operational by the criteria of the Turing test. What does this mean in terms of the child's intelligence?

At first, one is inclined to say that children are only as intelligent as they are capable of demonstrating alone, without the technological aid supplied by the computer. But this will not do. The reason is that this technological aid is similar to other aids that we readily allow and would never rip away from the child in our crudest assessments of a child's solo intelligence: such symbol systems as written language and mathematics. These systems are truly technologies, as are the symbolic artifacts of computer programs. If the child can use the computer symbol system as an aid in solving complex problems, it should be just as admissible as the thinking tools provided by written language (for example, by note taking during arithmetic calculations, or by list making in a formal operational experiment). Like mathematical and language notation, the symbolic notations used in the computational environment provide a powerful means for the child's thinking.

The consequences of these integrations are profound for developmentalists (including Piaget) bound to the assessment of intelligence in solitary settings. We should consider what these new possibilities say about stage conceptions of human intellectual development. What types of problems will emerge in the student modelling necessary for integrating computer and human intelligence, and for developing usable programs from the child's perspective? As intelligent systems become widely available, what are the implications for the emergence of highly creative mental acts in the arts and sciences throughout society? What complex ethical problems will be raised by such fusions?

Systems for the Coevolution of Human-Computer Intelligence. Tikhomirov (1981) has asked the profound question of how the mediation of mental processes by computer differs from mediation by signs. For example, does the computer introduce qualitatively different changes into the structure of intellectual processes? And how can a new stage be distinguished in the development of human mental processes?

The most speculative but also the most spectacular possibility is that human and computer intelligence will coevolve. Perhaps only by joining the strengths of human intelligence with the strengths of the computer can the potential of either be realized. It will soon be necessary for any theory of learning and development to explain not only human or computer learning (Michalski and others, 1983) and development but also their symbiotic union. This speculative discussion casts aside reservations about the need for human self-sufficiency in intellectual functioning, because integration between human and computer intelligence will be the norm in future decades. Just as the human body is no longer the major tool for physical labor, and just as a carpenter need not use only hand tools, so will mental functioning no longer be the sole province of the human mind.

To carry this speculation further, we can submit that computers will not always be so obviously external to humans in their functioning as mental tools as they now are. They may ultimately be use-transparent and serve as literal organs of intelligence, even to the extent of being integrated with the physical confines of the body, if we so desire. Hardware differences between the machinery of the mind and of the computer will be glossed over, and integration on the physical level will characterize human-computer intelligent systems. The insight comes from cognitive science: Intelligence does not need human hardware (the nervous system) to run; it is independent of hardware. The consequence is that an intelligence system (that is, a system that has the programs needed for achieving intelligent performances) need not be based in the nervous system. Until recently, we have conceived of human intelligence (realized through the nervous system) and artificial intelligence (realized through microcircuitry) as distinct. But, these two intelligences can in principle be integrated, since the hardware differences need not serve as a barrier for a new hybrid intelligence. Already, microprocessors have been integrated with artificial limbs to provide a form of internal integration of human-computer systems. Of course, there are caveats: Complex ethical issues of personal identity, rights, and dominion will emerge. But, we cannot begin such discourse without charting the possibilities.

It is important to observe that computers, as components of such systems, can serve to bootstrap human intellectual development under human control and choice. Just as adults have been able to solve complex problems with computers that they were unable to before, so children should be able to go beyond their current developmental capabilities with computer assistance. Human-computer intelligence systems will serve to extend and ultimately to reorganize what we think of as human imagination, intelligence, problem-solving skills, and memory.

Conclusions

As Tikhomirov (1981) reminds us, the computer only creates possibilities for human development, to be realized when certain technical, psychological, and social conditions are met. While I have argued that we have the technical capabilities needed for integrating human and computer intelligence, there are few exemplars to demonstrate that the psychological conditions of effective integration have been met. And, social conditions have not been adequately considered. What are the goals for computer use in our society?

One consequence of the information age is that what children will need to know to learn and develop will be drastically different from what our educational system now provides. Today, we spend decades learning the three Rs and memorizing facts that are often already out-dated. A culture pervaded by AI-based developmental tools for all the basics, and also thinking tools in creative processes (such as design and invention) will lead to new definitions of intelligence. These definitions may highlight the skills that have long been the aim of a liberal arts education. Cognitive skills of information management; strategies for problem solving that cut across domains of knowledge; such meta-cognitive skills as planning, monitoring, and learning how to learn; and communication and critical inquiry skills will come to be valued more highly. Teaching the basic facts of the disciplines will not only not provide for an educated citizenry that can use the thinking tools of this age, but it will not even be feasible because of the information explosion.

In this chapter, there has been little opportunity to address the tough research questions that must be raised if we are to achieve success in the various levels of integration of human and computer intelligence. Developmental research is needed to elaborate the theory of cognitive tasks, the theory of stages of competence by domain, and the theory of interventions and stage transitions (Resnick, 1984) integral to the creation of computer-based developmental tools. Too little is known about how stages of knowledge are transcended to become new and more adequate constructs. Also, we know little about the expert teaching that we hope such systems would model, although substantial progress has been made in unpacking procedures of inquiry teaching or Socratic dialogue (Collins and Stevens, 1982; Arons, 1984).

This enterprise will depend on interdisciplinary collaborative work among the computer and cognitive scientists who build AI systems and the developmental psychologists, content area specialists, and educators who know so much about how the work and play of learning and development take place. Such groups can together study learning and developmental processes while simultaneously providing tools to transform the very activities of learning and development. There are no precedents. The printing press had profound cognitive and social consequences, especially in education (Eisenstein, 1979), but its effect will not compare with the consequences of interactive information tools that function with the basic currency of human thought processes, the symbol.

References

Arons, A. B. "Computer-Based Instructional Dialogs in Science Courses." *Science,* 1984, *224,* 1051–1956.

Barr, A., Bennett, J., and Clancey. W. *Transfer of Expertise: A Theme for AI Research.* Working Paper HPP–79–11. Stanford, Calif.: Heuristic Programming Project, Stanford University, 1979.

Barr, A., and Feigenbaum, E. A. (Eds.). *The Handbook of Artificial Intelligence*. Vol. 2. Los Altos, Calif.: William Kaufmann, 1982.

Boden, M. A. *Piaget*. Glasgow, Scotland: Fontana, 1979.

Boyle, C. F., and Anderson, J. R. "Acquisition and Automated Instruction of Geometry Proof Skills." Paper presented at the annual meetings of the American Educational Research Association, New Orleans, La., April 1984.

Brown, A. L. "Learner Characteristics and Scientific Texts." Paper presented at the annual meetings of the American Educational Research Association, New Orleans, La., April 1984.

Brown, A. L., Bransford, J. D., Ferrara, R. A., and Campione, J. C. "Learning, Remembering, and Understanding." In J. H. Flavell and E. M. Markman (Eds.), *Handbook of Child Psychology*. Vol. 3: *Cognitive Development*. New York: Wiley, 1983.

Brown, J. S. "Process Versus Product: A Perspective on Tools for Communal and Informal Electronic Learning." In *Report from the Learning Lab: Education in the Electronic Age*. New York: Educational Broadcasting Corporation, 1984.

Brown, J. S., Burton, R., and de Kleer, J. "Pedagogical, Natural Language, and Knowledge Engineering Techniques in SOPHIE I, II, and III." In D. Sleeman and J. S. Brown (Eds.), *Intelligent Tutoring Systems*. New York: Academic Press, 1982.

Bruner, J. S. *The Process of Education*. Cambridge, Mass.: Harvard University Press, 1960.

Burton, R. "Diagnosing Bugs in a Simple Procedural Skill." In D. Sleeman and J. S. Brown (Eds.), *Intelligent Tutoring Systems*. New York: Academic Press, 1982.

Carey, S. "Cognitive Development: The Descriptive Problem." In M. S. Gazzaniga (Ed.), *Handbook of Cognitive Neuroscience*. New York: Plenum, 1984.

Case, R. *Intellectual Development: From Birth to Adulthood*. New York: Academic Press, 1985.

Collins, A., and Stevens, A. L. "Goals and Strategies of Inquiry Teachers. " In R. Glaser (Ed.), *Advances in Instructional Psychology*. Vol. 2. Hillsdale, N.J.: Erlbaum, 1982.

Davis, R., and Lenat, D. B. *Knowledge-Based Systems in Artificial Intelligence*. New York: McGraw-Hill, 1981.

Dennett, D. C. *Brainstorms*. Montgomery: Vt.: Bradford, 1978.

diSessa, A. "Phenomenology and the Evolution of Intuition." In D. Gentner and A. Stevens (Eds.), *Mental Models*. Hillsdale, N.J.: Erlbaum, 1983.

Donaldson, M. *Children's Minds*. Cambridge, Mass.: Harvard University Press, 1978.

Eisenstein, E. L. *The Printing Press as an Agent of Change*. New York: Cambridge University Press, 1979.

Feigenbaum, E. A., and McCorduck, P. *The Fifth Generation: Artificial Intelligence and Japan's Computer Challenge to the World*. Reading, Mass.: Addison-Wesley, 1983.

Feldman, D. H. *Beyond Universals in Cognitive Development*. Norwood, N.J.: Ablex, 1980.

Feldman, D. H. "A Developmental Framework for Research with Gifted Children." In D. H. Feldman (Ed.), *Developmental Approaches to Giftedness and Creativity*. New Directions for Child Development, no. 17. San Francisco: Jossey-Bass, 1982.

Fischer, K. W. "A Theory of Cognitive Development: The Control and Construction of Hierarchies of Skills." *Psychological Review*, 1980, *87*, 477–531.

Friedland, P. E. *Knowledge-Based Experiment Design in Molecular Genetics*. Report No. 79–711. Stanford, Calif.: Computer Science Department, Stanford University, 1979.

Gardner, H. *Frames of Mind: The Theory of Multiple Intelligences*. New York: Basic Books, 1983.

Gentner, D., and Stevens, A. (Eds.). *Mental Models*. Hillsdale, N.J.: Erlbaum, 1983.

Hayes-Roth, F., Waterman, D., and Lenat, D. (Eds.). *Building Expert Systems*. Reading, Mass.: Addison-Wesley, 1984.

Kahnemann, D., Slovic, P., and Tversky, A. (Eds.). *Judgement Under Uncertainty: Heuristics and Biases.* New York: Cambridge University Press, 1982.

Laboratory of Comparative Human Cognition. "Culture and Cognitive Development." In W. Kessen (Ed.), *Handbook of Child Psychology.* Vol. 1: *History, Theory, and Methods.* New York: Wiley, 1983.

Langley, P., Ohlsson, S., and Sage, S. *A Machine Learning Approach to Student Modeling.* Technical Report CMU–RI–TR–84–7. Pittsburgh, Pa.: Robotics Institute, Carnegie-Mellon University, 1984.

Lindsay, R., Buchanan, B. G., Feigenbaum, E. A., and Lederberg, J. *DENDRAL.* New York: McGraw-Hill, 1980.

Luria, A. R. *Cognitive Development: Its Cultural and Social Foundations.* Cambridge, Mass.: Harvard University Press, 1976.

Michalski, R. S., Carbonell, J. G., and Mitchell, T. M. (Eds.). *Machine Learning: An Artificial Intelligence Approach.* Palo Alto, Calif.: Tioga, 1983.

Minsky, M. "Why People Think Computers Can't." *Technology Review,* 1983, *86* (6), 65–81.

Nisbett, R. E., and Ross, L. *Human Inference: Strategies and Shortcomings of Social Judgment.* Englewood Cliffs, N.J.: Prentice-Hall, 1980.

Olson, D. R., and Bruner, J. S. "Learning Through Experience and Learning Through Media." In D. R. Olson (Ed.), *Media and Symbols: The Forms of Expression, Communication, and Education.* Chicago: University of Chicago Press, 1974.

Ong, W. J. *Orality and Literacy: The Technologizing of the Word.* New York: Methuen, 1982.

Palincsar, A. S., and Brown, A. L. "Reciprocal Teaching of Comprehension-Fostering and Comprehension-Monitoring Activities." *Cognition and Instruction,* 1984, *1,* 117–175.

Papert, S. *Mindstorms: Children, Computers, and Powerful Ideas.* New York: Basic Books, 1980.

Piaget, J. *The Psychology of Intelligence.* Totowa, N.J.: Littlefield, Adams, 1960.

Piaget, J. *The Biology and Knowledge.* London: Routledge & Kegan Paul, 1971.

Piaget, J. "Intellectual Evolution from Adolescence to Adulthood." *Human Development,* 1972, *15,* 1–12.

Piaget, J. *The Child and Reality: Problems of Genetic Psychology.* New York: Grossman, 1973.

Piaget, J. *The Grasp of Consciousness.* London: Routledge & Kegan Paul, 1976.

Piaget, J. "Piaget's Theory." In W. Kessen (Ed.), *Handbook of Child Psychology.* Vol. 1: *History, Theory, and Methods.* New York: Wiley, 1983.

Resnick, L. B. "Toward a Cognitive Theory of Instruction." In S. Paris, G. Olson, and H. Stevenson (Eds.), *Learning and Motivation in the Classroom.* Hillsdale, N.J.: Erlbaum, 1984.

Rogoff, B., and Lave, J. (Eds.). *Everyday Cognition: Its Development in Social Context.* Cambridge, Mass.: Harvard University Press, 1984.

Rogoff, B., and Wertsch, J. V. (Eds.). *Children's Learning in the "Zone of Proximal Development."* New Directions for Child Development, no. 23. San Francisco: Jossey-Bass, 1984.

Scribner, S. "Modes of Thinking and Ways of Speaking: Culture and Logic Reconsidered." In P. N. Johnson-Laird and P. C. Wayson (Eds.), *Thinking: Readings in Cognitive Science.* New York: Cambridge University Press, 1977.

Shortliffe, E. H. *Computer-Based Clinical Therapeutics: MYCIN.* New York: American Elsevier, 1976.

Shweder, R. S. (Ed.). *Fallible Judgment in Behavioral Research.* New Directions for Methodology of Social and Behavioral Science, no. 4. San Francisco: Jossey-Bass, 1980.

Siegler, R. S. "Information-Processing Approaches to Development." In W. Kessen (Ed.), *Handbook of Child Psychology.* Vol. 1: *History, Theory, and Methods.* New York: Wiley, 1983.

Simon, H. A. "What Computers Mean for Man and Society." *Science,* 1977, *195,* 1186–1191.

Sleeman, D., and Brown, J. S. (Eds.). *Intelligent Tutoring Systems.* New York: Academic Press, 1982.

Stefik, M. J., and de Kleer, J. "Prospects for Expert Systems in CAD." *Computer Design,* April 21, 1983, pp. 65–76.

Stevens, A. L., Collins, A., and Goldin, S. "Misconceptions in Students' Understanding," *International Journal of Man-Machine Studies,* 1979, *11,* 145–156.

Tikhomirov, O. K. "The Psychological Consequences of Computerization." In J. V. Wertsch (Ed.), *The Concept of Activity in Soviet Psychology.* New York: M. E. Sharpe, 1981.

Turing, A. M. "Computing Machinery and Intelligence." *Mind,* 1950, *59,* 433–460.

Vygotsky, L. S. *Mind in Society: The Development of the Higher Psychological Processes.* Cambridge, Mass.: Harvard University Press, 1978.

Waldrop, M. M. "The Necessity of Knowledge." *Science,* 1984, *223,* 1279–1282.

Wason, P. C., and Johnson-Laird, P. N. *Psychology of Reasoning: Structure and Content.* Cambridge, Mass.: Harvard University Press, 1972.

Roy D. Pea is senior research scientist and associate director at the Center for Children and Technology, Bank Street College, New York City. His current work involves research and software tool development for teaching general problem-solving skills to children, and theoretical work on new methods and aims for education in an information age.

*Can computers teach about what it means to know
and make us better learners?*

Learning About Knowing

Andrea A. diSessa

There has been a great deal of conjecture in recent years that higher levels of cognitive activity are important in learning and intellectual development. Terminology and emphasis vary widely — problem solving (Newell and Simon, 1972; Tuma and Reif, 1980), heuristics (Polya, 1945; Schoenfeld, 1980), planning (Pea, 1982; Miller, 1979), metacognitive development (Kohlberg, 1964; Perry, 1970). Yet, the broadbrush view is the same. During the development of expertise and mature intellectual performance, one sees the acquisition not only of traditional subject matter and related skills but also of more general attitudes, patterns of behavior, or knowledge that often seems to be useful across much broader, even subject-independent, ranges. To varying degrees, one can see the target of this knowledge as intellectual functioning and knowledge itself. Thus, planning is about organizing one's own intellectual resources efficiently. Metacognition is about what people know about their own thinking processes.

Though some of this work is couched in terms of developmental stages with little attempt or no expectation of hastening learning, one of

I am grateful to S. Papert for originally turning my attention to these issues and to my students for allowing me to eavesdrop on their thinking. This paper has benefited from comments by M. diSessa, H. Ginsburg, T. Globerson, E. Klein, and L. Schauble. Support from the Spencer Foundation for the interview studies helped greatly.

E. L. Klein (Ed.). *Children and Computers.* New Directions for
Child Development, no. 28. San Francisco: Jossey-Bass, June 1985.

97

the most exciting educational implications is the leverage that one may expect by enhancing learning at these levels. Indeed, concern for these levels of understanding has extended beyond the research community to the point that, for example, the National Science Board's Commission on Precollege Education in Mathematics, Science, and Technology (1983) cites abstract problem solving along with science, mathematics, and technology as high-priority targets in efforts to improve our nation's educational system. Computers, and particularly programming, are frequently cited as important carriers of these skills.

Despite a relatively rich research history, no consensus has evolved as to the nature of higher-level knowledge, and despite optimism and enthusiastic efforts in courses and books (Rubinstein, 1980; Wickelgren, 1974), I believe it is fair to say that no compelling analysis and evidence have been offered to show exactly how high-level knowledge functions in human learning or problem solving, nor has there been a convincing demonstration of the general value of teaching to these levels. Heuristics, for example, is an attractive device for teaching some parts of mathematics, but it still remains clear that the greatest leverage in getting students to solve problems in science or mathematics more broadly lies in getting them to understand the subject matter involved, not in organizing their methods of attack on problems in general.

The intent of this chapter is to open up a class of higher-level knowledge in the area of the learning of science, specifically of physics, that previous research has all but ignored. The class is higher-level in that it is knowledge about physics knowledge rather than about physics per se. One might appropriately (though for historical reasons perhaps misleadingly) call such knowledge metaphysics. Coming at it from a slightly different direction, we can call this class of knowledge intuitive epistemology — assumptions that students make about the nature of knowledge and knowing that may affect what they actually pay attention to and do in acquiring knowledge. My claim is that students have such assumptions, that these assumptions can influence what they do in relatively dramatic ways so as to affect both how efficiently and what in particular they learn. In contrast to planning or problem solving, intuitive epistemology should be expected to exhibit itself more over the long-term scales of learning a subject than in the course of solving single problems. In fact, the educational leverage of intuitive epistemology can be expected most over these time scales and in learning rather than in direct transfer to a range of problem-solving situations. (I do not mean to rule out broad transfer, but this will be discussed later.)

Intuitive epistemology will be approached in three ways in this chapter. First, I will describe a theoretical frame for understanding what kind of knowledge system it is. This frame comes from a more extensive body of work done on intuitive conceptions on the level of content, intuitive physics. The second approach will be empirical, since it involves a pair of case studies of students learning physics that indicate some of the essential conjectured phenomenology of intuitive epistemology. Finally, I will take an extended look at how computation can be a substantial catalyst in developing more effective epistemological outlooks in our students.

Naive Physics

It has increasingly become apparent that the learning of physics does not take place on a blank slate but in the context of a rich and remarkably robust intuitive physics that often causes persistent difficulties in learning the real physics. The difficulties come from largely untaught notions that may conflict with textbook physics or that articulate the world in a way that is nearly incompatible with textbook physics.

According to diSessa (1981, 1983), intuitive physics is a rich and systematic, though hardly deductive or theory-like, collection of knowledge elements. A very prominent category of elements consists of phenomenological primitives, *p-prims* for short, which are relatively minimal abstractions of common events that serve as essentially self-explanatory analyses in thinking about the physical world. These are little scenarios that happen, in the eyes of the naive physicist, simply because "that's the way the world works." Thus, they are the intuitive equivalent of physical laws. "Things move in the direction you push them"; "a force that encounters resistance results in reduced effect"; "motion dies away"; "pushing an object off center spins it"; "immobile objects block (stop or deflect) mobile ones."

Besides being phenomenological (that is, being minimal abstractions of experienced reality) and essentially primitive (that is, possessing little explicit justification structure), elements of intuitive knowledge are graded, in the sense that some are much more prominent in the system than others. In fact, one can distinguish two qualities of this grading or priority structure: Cuing priority—how quickly or directly a knowledge element is evoked in a given context—and reliability priority—how resistant to being superseded or rejected an element is once activated. The development of intuitive physics during instruction is in large part a shifting and rearrangement of these priorities according to how useful the elements are in the developing physical knowledge system. For example, anthropomorphic attributions to the physical world, like intention, lose reliability as ways of thinking about the physical world. In contrast, heuristic expectations that things like effort and energy (understood in an intuitive sense) are conserved become refined and built into first-rank physical principles like conservation of energy.

Intuitive physics often behaves locally like a physical theory, in that it can provide the basis for predictions; a situation may match a p-prim or some configuration of p-prims well enough that certain behavior is directly prescribed. It can also provide the basis for explanations in terms of the perceived p-prim, albeit never with any very deep or complex justification. Indeed, these predictions and explanations are doubly weak in that the attachment of a p-prim to a situation is essentially at the level of recognition; little or no justification for application to the context can be provided, and most p-prims are heuristic in the sense that it is no occasion for great surprise when one fails to predict or explain. The robustness of intuitive physics is a matter of systemwide reinforcement, not the strength of belief in individual elements. This particular point is further elaborated and supported in diSessa and Globerson (1984).

Since intuitive physics is better established, my hope is to use it as a large-scale metaphor that can guide the analysis and investigation of intuitive epistemology. Thus, I propose to find a rather large vocabulary system of graded, relatively self-explanatory elements that derive from nearly superficial abstractions. The primary difference is that intuitive epistemology is a phenomenology of personal functioning; it consists of abstractions about one's own knowing and learning rather than about the physical world. In other ways, I conjecture that intuitive epistemology should display, in the large, the same patterns as intuitive physics. In particular, it should exhibit the properties of theories of knowledge and action in many instances, like heuristics or planning strategems, but in detail it should behave and develop like a robust-in-the-large, flimsy-in-the-small system: Each knowledge element may possess little generality (breadth of cuing) and little individual persuasive power (reliability), but on the whole the system may exhibit considerable robustness. The next section contains the empirical core of this chapter: case studies of two students who gave repeated evidence of possessing elaborate intuitive epistemologies that demonstrably affected what they paid attention to and did to acquire their physics knowledge.

Two Epistemologies

Both students in this study were bright, successful, and relatively articulate. Both were M.I.T. freshmen and part of an intensive study of their intuitive physics that afforded an hour per week of open-ended discussion and problem solving during the course of a semester. At the same time, both were taking freshman physics and a computer projects course, the latter under my direction. As it turned out, having these students in my course afforded me a useful second view into the natural functioning of their epistemologies.

Despite their academic similarities, these students showed remarkably contrasting epistemologies. One appears to be a version of the traditional view — that the learning of physics is a matter of acquiring new knowledge specifically located in the laws, principles, and equations of textbooks; the process is understood essentially as one of knowing the principles by name and statement and the equations by the letter. The other epistemology appears to be in some important respects a version of the view represented earlier — that the learning of physics intimately involves a substantial reorganization of intuition.

A "Results Man." Student A's first interview offered very clear evidence that he made observations about personal functioning like the minimal abstractions proposed to be at the root of intuitive knowledge. Even more clearly, he appeared on the surface to have strong assumptions about the nature of physical knowledge.

The interview began with a discussion of the physics course in which A was then enrolled. When queried about how he was enjoying the lecturer, A responded that he liked him reasonably well but that the lecturer spent too much time on derivations. A said that he was a "results man" and that he didn't really care how they were gotten. He said the derivations were "boring," and he didn't even listen to them. 'It is, after all, the results that are important.' (Paraphrases will be enclosed in single quotes.) I asked A in several different ways why he supposed that the lecturer included derivations. At first, he said he had no idea. But, when he was pushed, he suggested that it was possibly for historical interest or for "motivation." Motivation turns out to be a systematic excuse that A used to justify others' doing a class of things for which his core epistemology could see no use. Such excuses I take as low-reliability primitives, which nonetheless serve an important function in preserving the plausibility of his higher-reliability notions in the face of situations that cannot be understood on the basis of the core.

A was then asked to solve a physics problem that involved him in a conflict over which of two equations for potential energy he knew actually applied: $P.E. = mgh$ or $P.E. = GMm/r$. The conflict was acute, since the answer to the problem depended critically on the potential energy function. A became frustrated, especially as it became clear that he had not enough understanding of the different equations to decide which one applied. Finally, A declared, "Gee, maybe that's why I should pay attention to derivations."

Indeed, applicability conditions are one of the most important reasons why the qualitative knowledge involved in derivations is useful. A simply did not pay attention to that kind of knowledge; he seemed initially to have no way of understanding why it was important, and, not surprisingly, this epistemological position kept him from learning that sort of thing. What is especially interesting is A's apparent abstraction of the difficulties encountered in solving the problem and his proposing that derivational knowledge might be important for that. I thought that such an observation was extremely important and that it would undermine his results orientation. However, as interviews through the term proved, his results epistemology proved too well entrenched.

The computer projects course that I gave in which A was enrolled emphasized qualitative knowledge and intuitive understanding. As part of the course work, I asked students to do a research project. A's project was one that I had suggested in class; it involved finding a strategy for using fuel that optimized the height obtained from a rocket firing. It turns out that in many cases the optimal strategy is very simple: to use fuel as quickly as possible. I gave a proof in class that this was true in the simplest case, constant gravitational force. The proof was rigorous but qualitative. It involved no equations. Appendix 1 gives the proof.

A built a computer simulation, then began to experiment with a slightly more general case for the rocket problem: gravity decreasing according to the Newtonian $1/r^2$. His simulation uniformly gave the numerical result that the same strategy (quickest burn) worked in this case as well. At the same time, he tried various strategies to solve analytically for the height, but he did not succeed, and I was certain that the solution was beyond his technical sophistication. I could see that there was a slight extension to my in-class proof that applied to this situation, reminded A of the proof, and suggested that he try to do something similar for this new case.

A returned with more numbers from his simulation. I showed him the proof in the simple situation again. Then I told him directly that it was doable in this situation as well and that that should be the focus of his effort to finish the project. In the preliminary draft of his final report, A again produced numbers and graphs but no qualitative analysis. Almost in desperation, I wrote a step-by-step sketch of the proof, even though it was not excessively difficult, and asked him to fill in the details.

When he turned in his final report, A told me he has "gotten it." I concluded that he had finished the proof and seen what was going on. On inspection, however, I discovered that what he meant was that he had improved his simulation to the point that he firmly believed the small numbers he was getting. The proof sketch was present but not elaborated over the form I had given him.

Though this instance is particularly striking, such a refusal or inability to deal qualitatively with physics was not limited to this single episode. For example, in trying to solve an even more complicated situation with the rocket adding friction, A found that the previously optimal strategy apparently did not get the best results. It was clear to me that, though he had only managed to show a numerically tiny failure, if he picked an extreme case (large friction) it would be easy for him to see why the strategy failed. I remarked that the discrepancy was small, near the limits of his simulator, and encouraged him to try to find a situation where the failure was clear. A continued to focus on numerical results, taking more and more data from test firings and continuing to get the small discrepancy. He never sought to optimize the discrepancy, nor did he seek, as far as I could see, to see why the strategy failed (a necessarily qualitative pronouncement) so that he could exaggerate the failure.

During his final interview, I asked A how he had liked the seminar. He said it was fine but that I had placed too much emphasis on qualitative understanding. He told me he understood that it was important for motivation but that you also need to get to the "real results."

In summary, A had a systematic view of physics that the knowledge resides in the equations and numbers. He prized results and viewed qualitative knowledge with suspicion. Indeed, he could not be persuaded that a nonanalytic argument could be conclusive, and he gave no indication that he had any sense of improving or finishing such an argument.

"Real Understanding." In contrast, B scarcely ever mentioned equations while solving physics problems. A and many other students like him frequently say something like "I'm trying to think of the equation" when they find themselves in a tight squeeze with a problem. I have often had students maintain that they could not solve a problem

because they could not remember the equation, even though it was clear to me that they were confused or stuck for quite other reasons. My offering to tell them any equation they could describe to me has never disrupted the pattern. These students apparently focus on their only or at least on their most prominent model of physical knowledge when their problem solving fails. Naturally, any attempt to remember the equation in such circumstances is simply time wasted. When I queried B about the fact that he scarcely ever mentioned equations, he said he just never thought about them: "They just seem to 'pop up' when I need them, when I've finally figured out what's going on in the problem."

B had an explicit view of the problem-solving process. He maintained that the most interesting and important part lies in figuring out what is going on in the situation; then you can write down equations to solve, and finally you have to go back and see what the numbers you get mean. The last step he justified partially as a check to see whether the numbers made sense, but, more important, he maintained that solving a problem means figuring out something about the world, not "getting a number." Since some of this sounded extremely professional, I asked him whether he had read anything about problem solving. His reply was that he had heard of "that kind of stuff" but that he hadn't been taught and that he hadn't read anything about it.

B was aware that certain exercises contained conceptual difficulties rather than just numerical or other superficial complexities. He stated that he "collected" such problems and that he worked them through when he had time. On another occasion, he stated that he always tried to work through a problem "intuitively" first, then, after he had worked through the details, he would compare his intuition with the detailed answer he was sure of in order to 'save the good intuitions and find out the bad ones.'

It is, of course, possible to underestimate the power of equations and other formal methods. I have encountered several students who almost refused to grant any understanding status at all to equations, thus handicapping themselves in improving their intuitions. Such students, at least at M.I.T., seem very rare. B did not have this problem, as evidenced by his use of problem solutions to prune and refine his intuitions.

B had a very well-developed esthetic sense for what he considered "real understanding." He would often comment about things he really understood and about things that made sense that he didn't really understand. Unfortunately, his criteria for what real understanding was never explicitly became a topic of conversation. Even if they had, I expect that the internal phenomenology would be very difficult to describe. Many of his attempts to describe the problem-solving process in detail indicated that he had such a phenomenology but that it proved very difficult to articulate. For example: 'Well, you sometimes just jump ahead (an insight?), and then fill in the gaps.' Yet his commitment to real understanding was strong. During one interview, he spent an extended period of time complaining that he had so much work at M.I.T. that he never had the time to really understand the material. He was very worried about what that would do to his sense of understanding during the course of his four years at M.I.T. As a researcher, he believed that sensing the weak parts of his understanding would be a vital part of the job.

As it turned out, B's project was one of the best I have ever had in the projects course. He discovered what to my knowledge was an unknown phenomenon, conducted a thorough empirical investigation of it, and finally gave a qualitative and essentially correct explanation for it. Unfortunately, I did not have enough contact with the development of his project to be able to relate that success to elements of his intuitive epistemology.

There were some detectable faults in B's epistemology from my perspective, but often he produced exceptionally well-founded thinking and learning phenomenology and strategies for dealing with it. He had an explicit concern for developing qualitative understanding in the short term and intuitive knowledge in the longer term. He downplayed, perhaps to an extreme, the value of formulas, and he cultivated and valued a sense of graded understanding.

Extending the Context

In view of the limited empirical base, I will make some attempt in this section to note the gaps and establish a broader context.

The Edges of the Intuitive Physics Metaphor. I began setting a context for intuitive epistemology by proposing a large-scale metaphor with a domain that is better understood: intuitive physics. Though what we have seen so far is consistent with the general outline of intuitive physics, including a richness of phenomenology perceived by students sufficient to constitute the basis for an intuitive epistemology, it is clear that we must expect limitations in the metaphor. Knowledge about the physical world is one of the most important and hence one of the richest parts of human experience. Five senses are devoted to it (though, for intuitive physics, no doubt sight and touch dominate). We cannot expect intuitive epistemology to be as rich and as integrated or to contain elements as highly reliable as naive physics does.

Natural language contains a rich commonsense vocabulary for the phenomena of the physical world. On the contrary, the phenomenology of knowledge is very subtle; a great deal of it rests on sensing states of the mind. It is difficult even to think of vocabulary describing it that is not in some way a metaphor drawn from the physical world: finding *support* for an argument, *retrieving* or *blocking on* a piece of information. Even these terms hardly do justice to the sensations of mental events that one wishes to describe.

Instruction never attacks intuitive epistemology in the way that formal physics offers a frame that competes with intuitive physics. So, we might not expect as much development or final results as systematic as the transition from naive to expert physical intuition. Indeed, the character of formal physics constrains and hints at the development of intuitive knowledge in ways that we simply do not have for intuitive epistemology. We must expect a slower development of our own understanding.

Development. These brief studies, chosen for their high contrast, may leave one with the impression of a good intuitive epistemology as a natural faculty or developmental stage. A, whose epistemology seems lacking and clearly dysfunctional, was not evidently helped by a course designed specifically to improve students' understanding of metaphysics. In contrast, B is clearly extraordinary as far as his epistemology is concerned; it seems unlikely on the face of it that we could intercede to improve his understanding given our own present understanding of profitable and unprofitable views of knowledge. But, our measures of epistemology are so feeble that seeing development over the course of four months is more than we could expect. Even if the course had planted the seeds to undermine A's "results" view (which, given our experience of the robustness of intuitive physics, should take a long time) and even if B's great success in the course reinforced his spontaneously developed ideas to the point where they could provide even greater leverage in learning, we have no way of knowing.

Along similar lines, it is possible to interpret aspects of intuitive epistemology as matters of intellectual style. A may simply need a different learning context that is supportive of his expectations and mode of thinking. In some respects, this must be true; it makes no sense to treat students with such radically different expectations in identical ways. Yet, I resist the temptation to think of these differences as intrinsic characteristics of individuals in any sense extending beyond the robustness that one seems to find in rich intuitive knowledge systems, again taking naive physics as a model. The strong claim I wish to make, if not to prove, here is that B simply knows some things that A does not. B has a view of knowledge that is much more consistent with the realities of coming to know physics than A's is. Implicitly, I am saying that A can and probably will learn those things. I will give some empirical support for such progression, which is not present in the case studies, in my description of another study in the next section.

Domain Independence. To what extent does the knowledge that I am discussing deserve the name intuitive epistemology and not metaphysics? That is, to what extent is it domain-independent knowledge? The case studies suggest that most of the relevant phenomenology comes from the students' problem solving and learning in physics per se. More than that, most of the points made were in line with my position on naive physics, namely that a proper intuitive epistemology for physics is in significant measure an appreciation of the values and dangers in one's own preexisting intuitive knowledge about the physical world. One cannot make that case so clearly for mathematics, nor would one expect the relationship between intuitive knowledge and less worldly mathematics to be nearly the same, even if it turns out to be as deep.

At the same time, it is not hard to see commonalities in coming to understand almost any scientific domain at the level of knowing what constitutes precise description, the integration of multiple representations, recognizing and cultivating highly reliable knowledge, the development of intuitive insight into respectable scientific understanding, and sophistication about the nature of explanation, demonstration, and proof.

The best guess that one can make at this point is to assume various degrees of overlap among the epistemologies appropriate to different scientific disciplines. Some domain dependencies might be so particular that the epistemological knowledge must be considered to be part of the field. But, even this special knowledge can be important in learning, say, physics, and it is currently left entirely out of the curriculum.

When considering the question of domain independence, it is enlightening to compare this work with a very substantial study of a different sort concerning intellectual development in the college years (Perry, 1970). Perry's explicit aim was to chart development in the general structures in terms of which university students view their intellectual experience during their four undergraduate years. His study was based on open-ended interviews and did not focus on the learning of any particular subject. What emerged was a clear-cut epistemological development starting with a simple, dichotomous right-wrong perspective, developing through a stage in which more complex criteria are recognized as necessary in assessing knowledge, and progressing finally to a stage where the student establishes necessary commitments in a world of many frames of reference and relative validity.

Perry had little difficulty getting his students to talk about these issues. Like A and B, they had a great deal to say about knowledge and knowing. But, the points of comparison between the present study and Perry's are sharpest in the actual statements of students. A constant theme in early stages of development is a search for right answers — A's "results" — and concomitant complaints that instructors hide the facts, like A's complaints about my qualitative point of view. "If teachers would stick more to the facts and do less theorizing, one could get more out of their classes. . . . A certain amount of theory is good, but it should not be dominant . . . the facts are what's *there*. And I think that should be . . . the main thing" (Perry, 1970, p. 67). Indeed, the students in Perry's study eventually found excuses for their professor's behavior, like A's "historical interest" and "motivation." A common reason attributed to instructors and books for not giving the "right answer" was that the students would have to figure it out for themselves.

Parallels between Perry's findings and mine are less salient for the more sophisticated students. To be sure, he saw a general appreciation for the complexities of knowing, and he found students at the highest levels talking in very nearly the same terms as he did about their epistemologies, like B and my view of intuitive physics. But, those terms centered on relativity and commitment (as characterized by Perry), not on levels of understanding, intuitive knowledge, and so on. The diminished parallelism might well be attributable to the liberal arts orientation of Perry's work; science courses are not mentioned except as places where "there is a formula" (note the metaphor) and "there are *facts*." But, a slight reinterpretation of Perry allows us to draw much more striking parallels. If one matches frames of reference with representational forms (numbers, equations, qualitative analysis) and commitment with the perception of an underlying invariance, then, despite the different vocabulary, there is considerable overlap between Perry's and my descriptions of the experience and function of a richer epistemology. Here, I am referring to B's use of both formal and informal representations of problems. A more extended discussion of representational sophistication appears in the next main section.

Children and Intuitive Epistemology. Many, including Perry, consider that metacognitive development begins around age fifteen. Others, such as Papert (1980), suggest that the issue is important for children. Papert also claims that children are capable of abstracting ideas about personal intellectual functioning from prominent activities in programming, like debugging, that can be generally useful in learning. In general, research in the area is scattered in perspective and results, and this is not the place for a review.

An anecdote helps to state my position: My seven-year-old son has been spending a fair amount of time trying to figure out why the moon appears to follow us when we drive in the car. At one point, he told me that he had "got it" the previous day "for just an instant," and then he forgot it. It is unlikely he would believe me if I told him that, whatever happened in that instant, it is extremely unlikely that he solved the problem. It is too complex and in other ways is simply not the kind of knowledge that one can get in an instant and then forget as quickly. Such events convince me that intuitive epistemology is a natural phenomenon in children as well as in young adults. What is even clearer is that elementary school science and mathematics programs, especially the latter, with their emphasis on algorithms and the rest, must provide very poor soil for good ideas about knowledge. But, saying more than that and speculating on the importance and teachability of such knowledge for children must be reserved for the future.

Engineering a Better Epistemology

Both A and B are abstracting on the basis of their educational experiences. A in particular, focused on prominent objects in his intellectual purview — numbers, equations, propositions, "results" — to organize his epistemology. These are not necessarily very prominent parts of a scientific education. If we changed A's experiences in a significant way, there is every reason to believe that he would develop a different epistemological position with more productive models of knowledge. In more general terms, if anything like the origin and developmental patterns sketched for intuitive physics hold for intuitive epistemology, there is no reason to believe in any developmental inevitability.

So, education may well be an application for what we learn about intuitive epistemology. At the same time, it may be a potent empirical medium. Indeed, without any developmental determinism, we almost necessarily find ourselves in a position of inventing epistemologies and of testing their learnability and profitability. Psychological research in a situation where considerable investment (such as developing a significant part of a subject's experience over a nontrivial time span) is necessary in order to achieve any reasonable effect, then amortizing that investment by simultaneously meeting other goals (like teaching a physics course) is necessary. The computer projects course referred to earlier in this chapter is being developed with explicit epistemological intentions. It is thus simultaneously a testing ground for the application of current ideas and an admittedly somewhat messy but provocative empirical medium for the development of new ones.

Techniques. Here I limit myself to a general description of methods and therefore to a plausibility argument that one can expect a computational context to have significant effects along the lines of the contrast between A and B if it is properly engineered and supported. I phrase these methods along four dimensions and take examples from the projects course. This is not to suggest that the computer by itself can induce change. On the contrary, if intuitive physics suggests one thing, it is that changes in knowledge systems like those I am describing need concerted, long-term effort in order to show stable influence. Computation must be integrated into a broad effort to change the perceived intellectual terrain. The conjecture is specifically that computation can be extraordinarily helpful in the context of this broad effort.

Amplifying Qualitative Methods. Equations provide a major attractor as a model for knowledge. They may be the single most prominent intellectual tool presented in high school and college-level science courses. Yet, for reasons evident in A's difficulties, they are rather a poor model of knowledge. Computation offers competing formalisms, most prominently programs themselves. In contrast to mere qualitative analysis, as might be demonstrated in text or lectures, these can be seen to do significant work, for example, in creating simulations. Trivial numerical algorithms can replace the manipulation of fancy equations and at the same time provide a conceptually clean model for the laws of physics. A simple example, the algorithmic version of Newton's first two laws, follows:

$$v: = v + (F/m)\Delta y$$
$$x: = x + v\Delta t$$

Here : = means that the new value of the quantity on the left is computed with the expression on the right. F is the force applied to the object, x is its coordinate position, v is velocity, m is the object's mass, and Δt is the time internal between computations of the new quantities. These relationships are usually represented by the equation $F = ma,$ where a is the acceleration of the object (that is, the time rate of change of velocity, $a = dv/dt$). The subsidiary relationship, $v = dx/dt,$ is assumed.

The algorithmic formulation expresses the fundamental laws in terms of a trivial formalism, arithmetic, rather than in terms of derivatives. The latter are best at the edges of a student's knowledge when physics is usually first taught. I have argued elsewhere (diSessa, 1979) that not only does this reduce the set of prerequisites for teaching physics, but the procedural nature of the algorithmic formulation increases the intuitive accessibility. More to the point in this context, three things are true of the algorithmic formulation:

- It supports simple abstraction of important qualitative dependencies. For example, position, x, is not changed directly by force, F. Instead, F changes an intermediate influence, v, which then changes position.
- It is evidently universal. Providing that F and initial x and v are specified, this algorithm directly solves the time development of any mechanical system. Thus, the universal nature of $F = ma$ is evident, not hidden by technical tricks necessary in special cases to solve analytically. From an epistemological point of view, it is fundamentally important to lay out the grading and conceptual dependencies of a knowledge system as cleanly as possible.
- It is constructive. The algorithm can be implemented as a program to simulate any forced motion. Not only does this reinforce the universal character of the law, but it opens up large areas of phenomenological exploration and experimentation.

More generally, programs to do simulation or analysis, even to manipulate the equations themselves, can demonstrate nonnumerical techniques, such as heuristic methods, trial and error, and even the manipulation of symbols and equations as objects. At their best, these methods are much better models of intellectual processes then equation solving as an unarticulated problem-solving skill. For example, one of the simulators provided in the computer projects course is a ray-tracing optics simulation that determines certain paths by guesswork and successive approximation rather than by analytic solution. A better example, though not used in this course, is a symbolic integration program that works not by strict algorithm but by explicitly looking for patterns heuristically suggestive of particular techniques.

It is, of course, important for students to build these programs themselves or at least to have occasion genuinely to consider how the programs work rather than merely to use them. Programming is standard practice in the projects course. Note that what is primarily important here is the notion of heuristic methods and heuristic methods as models of human intellectual activity, not the particular methods themselves. It is not likely that B would measure better than A on any test of specific heuristics. The important thing is an attitude that allows students to see, appreciate, and seek to add heuristic knowledge to their own repertoire.

This stance contrasts with most educational implementations of heuristic methods. Teaching specific heuristics might be an approach toward such an attitude, but it is not obviously the best one for two important reasons. Both have to do with lack of continuity with a student's state. First, as high-priority cleaned up and formalized entities, explicit heuristics bears little resemblance to the uncertain guesses and ways of thinking that are contiguous with a student's experienced intellectual world. It is not in any sense the minimal abstractions that I have conjectured intuitive epistemology to consist of. Second, heuristics is often difficult to make obviously powerful to the point where students attribute a specific and essential role to it in their own thought processes. Once again, the emphasis on using various nonanalytic strategies in programming is so that students can concretely see these as powerful.

Choosing a Different Class of Problems. Data on intuitive physics show that standard physics problems can prompt solution attempts that short-circuit conceptual engagement (Larkin and others, 1980). The phase of problem solving that B described as "figuring out what is going on" can thus be very much underpresented. In contrast, problems that are posed phenomenologically — for example, through dynamic presentation on a computer display screen — can highlight the process of converting from commonsense description to physical concepts. Not only is this process a legitimate part of learning to do physics, but any method of making it a more prominent part of the problem-solving process should contribute to better metalevel conceptions of the knowledge of physics as well. Though not necessarily a computer activity, problem-solving sessions built explicitly around problematic intuitive expectations can make vivid the kind of conceptual reorganization required to learn physics that, until recently, has not been understood, let alone been a significant target of physics instruction.

Time scale is an important parameter of the work that students are provided to exercise their developing understanding. I believe that the one hour per problem paradigm, which dominates current teaching practice, is deficient in at least two respects. Such work simply cannot reliably demonstrate within its natural bounds many of the key phenomena of coming to understand, such as the effect that a shift of perspective can have in understandability or even the central process of gradually building on an insight over an extended period of time to arrive first at partial, then at reliable and secure, understanding. It is important metaknowledge to know both how much work often needs to be done to achieve a seemingly small shift in perspective and how important that shift can be.

In mathematics instruction, short problems can never involve a student in inventing a definition in the way a mathematician does it. Mathematicians understand that definitions are made so that theorems can be proved, so that the theorem is true. Within a naive epistemological perspective, definitions are not negotiable in that way, nor is truth something that is created. In this regard, Lakatos (1976) provides clear descriptions of many mathematical processes involved in building a mathematical truth from failed attempts at proposing definitions and theorems. In physics, small problems can hardly establish the context for inventing a technique for solving a class of problems, and, particularly if the problems are only text-based, they can almost never let a student build a conjecture about an underlying mechanism out of phenomenological exploration.

These activities are part of the professional physicist's repertoire of activities. But, that is only a secondary motivation for finding ways of making them more prominent in a student's intellectual life. I believe that an esthetic sense concerning the building and functionality of scientific knowledge constitutes some of the best leverage in understanding even textbook presentations, such as what to look for in proofs and what to remember from techniques.

Teaching Different Subjects. Educators are used to thinking about selecting and ordering subjects into a curriculum on the basis of prerequisites and according to the value of the subject-level knowledge involved. Once one has a higher-level agenda, selection and ordering have other criteria. For example, one could argue that teaching Newtonian mechanics provides an excessively "clockwork" image of physics, nearly deductive in its character, in which every problem can be solved in closed form using a machinery, equation solving, that has problems as a model of understanding. One might well choose to postpone or spread out the teaching of Newtonian mechanics in favor of introducing subjects that provide better epistemological grist. Indeed, the projects course includes a unit on geometric optics simply because it is a very good domain for highlighting the value of incomplete but simple models.

As it happens, Newtonian mechanics can be adopted to this new pedagogical agenda. It offers significant opportunities for student projects and activities. Just as important, since the phenomena of intuitive physics are reasonably well studied and offer dramatic demonstrations of the nature of naive understanding, that topic can become an explicit part of the curriculum. More radically, the projects course contains a unit on an alternate formulation of Newtonian mechanics (diSessa, 1980) with very different connections to intuitive physics. This unit is taught along with the standard version for the epistemological points that can be made from a formally identical but very different feeling presentation.

In general, one looks for a shift toward subjects that allow significant research, exploration, and design in addition to problem solving.

The computer's role in supporting such a shift is multifaceted. Computation can directly present alternative realities for exploration. It can provide situations in which students do research by using and even building analytic tools and models and in other ways by constructing their own understanding schemes. As the computer has become an indispensable tool for data analysis, model building, and studying design alternatives by professionals, so it is nearly indispensable in similar work for students.

Eroding Naive Realism. A central goal of an epistemologically sound curriculum is to open up the learning and knowing process for students' inspection and to provide better concrete models for knowledge than simple knowing of results and equations. A very helpful step is to provide understanding in forms that are not to be confused with straightforward facts about the world. Such forms of knowledge evidently must be examined for their good and bad properties as ways of knowing, just as any human understanding must be examined. Intellectual model building becomes a central topic.

Computers can contribute to this goal in many ways. Not the least is the concrete way in which computers allow one to build models, as already mentioned. The geometric optics simulation, for example, is not properly a simulation at all but an explicit collection of models that can be compared with each other and with reality. Another simulation from the projects course used a quite clearly wrong law of motion to model stress and strain in bridges. Yet, in the context in which this law is used, it gives predictions about the breaking points of physical structures as precise and accurate as the correct law. Naive realism and an adherence to a unique way of understanding the world are challenged by such a simulation.

One of the profound notions of contemporary cognitive science is that of representation, which at its root concerns the symbolic encoding of knowledge. The computer has provided this idea with its impetus. Artificial intelligence is a new empirical science of mind based on the building of explicit and operational representations of knowledge. The conjecture here is that the notion of representation, supported by a computational context, can serve to open up understanding to close inspection and hence improve intuitive epistemology.

To support the case and exemplify the technique of using the notion of representation, consider the following simple turtle geometric definition of a circle:

REPEAT 360 [FORWARD 1 RIGHT 1]

The turtle is a graphics cursor that comes as part of the LOGO computer language and that can move and draw on a display screen (Abelson and diSessa, 1981; Papert, 1980). By moving forward a bit, reaiming with a small turn, and repeating over and over, the turtle generates a circle (Figure 1). If one runs such a program with a large distance in the FORWARD command (Figure 2a), the turtle marches off the edge of the computer screen and "wraps," jumping to the opposite border of the screen (dotted line) while maintaining its current heading. The striking fact is that, if one continues the circle program, it wraps repeatedly but returns precisely to its starting point after turning three-hundred-and-sixty degrees as if it had not wrapped at all (Figure 2b). To explain this is a problem we have posed as a standard part of a high school summer program, the precursor of the current physics projects course (Abelson and diSessa, 1976).

The point of interest is that the problem can be solved trivially by a shift in representation of the notion of wrapping. Instead of thinking of wrapping as an operation on the turtle as it reaches the edge of the screen, we can think of wrapping as an artifact of a peculiar way of viewing the turtle's walking on a place: Suppose we divide the plane into rectangles, each viewed by a television camera in such a way that the boundary of each camera's view matches the boundary of its rectangle. Suppose further that the signals from all the cameras are mixed so that what we see on the monitor is all the rectangles at once. With this set-up, what we see on the screen is identical to what we saw originally:

Figure 1. A Turtle Nearing the End of a Circle Walk

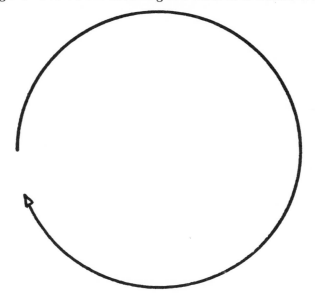

Figure 2a. The Dotted Line Represents the Turtle "Wrapping"

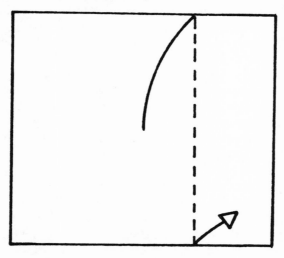

When the turtle crosses an edge, it disappears at the edge (from one camera's view) and reappears at the opposite edge (in another camera's view). But, the mysterious closure is now no more mysterious than the closure of the on-screen circle, since the turtle is actually marching in a circle on an ordinary plane.

The moral is that choosing an appropriate way of representing a situation can often be the most crucial step in understanding it. Like

Figure 2b. The Multiply Wrapped Circle Still Closes

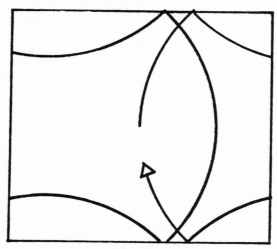

any isolated example, this one can serve only as a seed for convincing students of the utility of considering the character of and alternatives to any obvious way of understanding. Fortunately, this example is not isolated, in the sense that it provides a concrete image for a very general class of geometric representations. This class of representations not only provides insight, but also the capability to simulate various geometric worlds on a computer. Especially for students who have not built a personal appreciation for such concepts as qualitative knowledge, one must begin with ideas that are as evidently powerful as equations and numbers in a conventional physics course. Luckily, the notion of representation is indisputably powerful whenever one want to build part of the world into a computer program. I have taken an example that stands somewhat apart from physics, but the point is no different in physics. Indeed, it reinforces the conjecture that there is a core epistemology across scientific disciplines.

In the projects course, the theme of representation has a number of embodiments. First, it is a constant explicit and implicit issue when it comes time to build a model into a computer program. Second, examples like the one just given are built into the exposition. The qualitative proof given in Appendix 1 is another such example. Finally, the concept of an imagistic or physical representation is consistently used to force attention to meaning prior to and independent of such formalisms as mathematical quantities (numbers, vectors) and their relationships (equations). (Goldin, 1983, uses the term *imagistic representation* to describe a certain kind of nonverbal encoding of knowledge. There is a strong relationship between this encoding and intuitive physics as I describe it, but my intention in using the notion here is as a construction for educational consumption, not as a technical term for human cognition.) In small ways, this is usually done in physics courses. The notion of force is introduced as a push or a pull — common intuitive notions. What is essentially never done is to build such ideas into a qualitative formalism, in which the images are gradually refined and generalized to the point where they can serve as tools of analysis approaching the precision that we commonly expect of scientific ideas.

The concept of a qualitative formalism is difficult to exemplify in a short nontechnical exposition. Appendix 2 provides an example for readers who are up to high school or freshman physics. The essential point is simple. One needs to create explicit, named examples of ways of thinking that are rich, reliable, broadly or universally applicable, yet evidently built out of the materials everyone comes to a new subject with, intuition and common sense.

The Status of These Strategies. The strategies just discussed step rather brazenly beyond the bounds of the scientifically justified. Admittedly, they are drawn from a personal sense for good and bad intuitive epistemologies and for points of educational leverage, a sense developed in teaching physics and from interviews like those that allowed the case studies presented here. The notion of qualitative understanding, for example, has not yet been unpacked to the point that it is a legitimate technical term. One will eventually need better criteria than family resemblance to justify the inclusion of topics in an epistemological curriculum. The sense of grading (for example, the importance of the notion of representation) and plausible sequence implicitly demonstrated in examples will need to be elaborated in the same way that one always expects the curriculum of a new subject to be responsive to attempts to teach it and also to a developing sense for the internal logic of the curriculum.

Finally, an implicit strategic decision permeates the engineering section of this chapter. It is to teach epistemology largely by changing the way in which the subject is taught: what subtopics are taught, how they are explained, what activities students engage in. There are alternatives. One may branch off to a separate subject, as has happened with problem solving. One may take a historical perspective in teaching the subject, the so-called genetic approach, in which the human evolution of scientific knowledge can no doubt be made salient in some sense. One can teach a psychological epistemology explicitly, in as much as one knows this. For example, this chapter might be part of a course.

The choice of the present path over others is guided primarily by the fundamental conjecture that intuitive epistemology is built from self-made observations of the structure of knowledge and of personal intellectual functioning. Thus, I propose that the task is largely one of providing better models and experiences from which to abstract. To be sure, it is appropriate to teach some explicit notions and terminology. But, respecting the essentially personal nature of the construction of knowledge, it is never appropriate to separate the task of developing an epistemology from the context of building a functional knowledge system of the sort that justifies, in my view, the concern for epistemology at all.

Summary

Almost everyone is aware of a certain phenomenology of mental events and personal functioning. People know, to varying degrees, when they are confused, when they really understand, when they have lost track of an argument, when a text is literally understandable but written from a foreign perspective. Everyone has some sense for what an insight feels like; we may hope that they have abstracted both some general things to do when they get one and something that allows them to know when they are done testing and refining that insight. The first contention of this chapter is that this class of knowledge, which I call intuitive epistemology, exists and is important to learning.

Such an inarticulate knowledge system will be very difficult to study. But, some existing work on other intuitive knowledge systems suggests what to look for. One should expect a rather large and loosely coupled collection of minimal abstractions. An example of such abstraction that many psychologists recognize is the feeling of inevitable going backward on an apparent solution path that characterizes the trickiness of a class of puzzle problems exemplified by the famous missionaries and cannibals problem. Undoubtedly, many or even most such abstractions are of such low priority that they rarely enter into conscious consideration or choice of action.

The system as a whole, however, may well define a general stance toward knowledge that has significant consequences for which things are learned and which are not. The two case studies included here indicate that, sometimes at least, intuitive epistemology can crystallize into an apparently coherent point of view, including such relatively reliable (high-priority) and spontaneously generated concepts as results and figuring things out and a feeling for which knowledge is important and real. These views may be responsible for either a heightened focus or a profound misdirection with respect to some important features of scientific knowledge.

The second major contention of this chapter is that the computer can be a major tool in creating educational environments that support more sophisticated and productive epistemologies in our students. I have outlined a series of techniques by which computation can alter the activities and implicit or explicit concepts from which students abstract to form their views of knowledge. Prominent among these techniques are the concept of representation and the altering both of exposition and of the problems that students work on to better represent the quality of thinking and time scale of the phenomenology of coming to know.

It has often been said that computers can alter the way we think. But, for this grandiose claim to have substance, we need some sense for "better thinking" and ideas on how exactly it is that computers can do things for us in this regard. In this chapter I have sought to contribute to both these enterprises.

Appendix 1: A Qualitative Proof

Since much of my case concerning A's epistemology relies on his reaction to the qualitative proof of the quick burn strategy, it seems appropriate to lay it out for inspection. In addition, the proof is used in the projects course as an example of the technique of shifting representations to gain insight, a strategy suggested in the engineering section.

The Problem. A rocket has a fixed amount of fuel, but it can be programmed to use the fuel at any rate. For simplicity, consider a model of the engine such that the amount of force supplied is strictly proportional to the rate of use of the fuel. Thus, the amount of velocity acquired is proportional to the amount of fuel used. (Ignore the reduced mass of the rocket due to the use of fuel.) How should the fuel be used so that the rocket achieves maximum height? Conjecture: Burn the fuel as quickly as possible.

Constant Gravity. The case of constant gravity was examined in class. The key to proving the conjecture is to represent the problem through a velocity versus time graph. Figure 3 shows the case of all fuel burned at once. The rocket acquires a velocity, v, and is continuously decelerated by gravity (a straight line velocity graph corresponds to constant acceleration, which is constant gravity). The point of zero velocity is where the rocket stops moving upward, that is, the peak of its trajectory. The area under the velocity versus time graph to that point represents distance, the height achieved.

Now, if the rocket burns half its fuel, waits, then burns the rest, the graph appears as in Figure 4. In fact, the dotted line shown is the velocity graph for the first case, where all the fuel burned at once. If we

Figure 3. The Rocket's Velocity Versus Time Graph

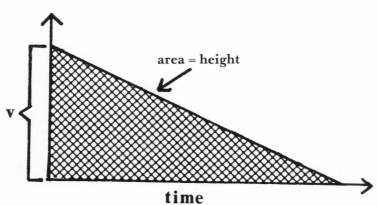

Figure 4. The Rocket's Velocity in the Second Case

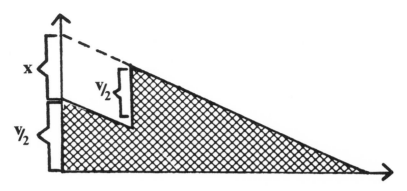

can prove this, the graphs for the two cases will be the same, except that the second case is missing the unshaded parallelogram area in Figure 4. This means that the second case achieves less height (less area) and in fact the defect compared with the first case is simply the area of the missing parallelogram.

To show that the dotted line is indeed the graph of the first case, note that all slanted sections, including the dotted one, have the same slope, which is the deceleration due to gravity. Since the missing area also has parallel (vertical) sides, it is a parallelogram; the segment, x, is therefore $v/2$. So the dotted line starts at $v/2 = v$ and slopes down at the same rate; it is the graph of the first case.

The generalization to arbitrary fuel use is trivial. In fact, the graph for velocity given any fuel use is always below the graph of the first case by precisely the velocity equivalent of the fuel not yet expended.

$1/r^2$ Gravity. Recall that A was shown the proof just given twice: once in class and once privately. He had not responded at all to the first suggestion that a similar proof would work for the $1/r^2$ case. At the second encounter regarding his project, A was told that the key to redoing the proof was that, since gravity decreased with distance, a rocket farther away from the earth (higher above it) will have a smaller deceleration. Thus the all-at-once case will be at an even greater advantage; having started faster and gained initial height advantage, its velocity graph will slope less steeply toward zero velocity.

The outline with which A was provided before his final paper included a diagram similar to Figure 5; again, it was remarked that the all-at-once case gained an additional advantage at the time shown from being at a greater height, because it thus decelerated more slowly. I leave it to the reader to refine this insight into a proof.

**Figure 5. The All-at-once Case Gets an Even Greater Advantage
Since Its Greater Initial Height Means Reduced Gravity,
Thus Decreased Deceleration (Slope)**

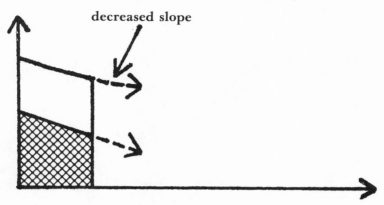

decreased slope

Appendix 2: A Qualitative Formalism

One of my favorite examples of qualitative formalism occurs in the study of rotational dynamics — spinning things. The image of an object turning around an axis turns out to be both intuitively accessible and sufficiently powerful to serve as the basis for a qualitative formalism. The key points follow.

Every motion of an object, once translation (motion from place to place) has been factored out, can be achieved as rotation around an axis. This means that the effect of any two successive rotations can be achieved as a single rotation about some third axis. This key theorem means that axis rotations are a universal way of thinking about rotations. It need not be proved to be understandable and useful. Indeed, though every standard treatment of rotational dynamics must implicitly use the theorem, it is essentially never stated.

The phenomenology of a general rotating system can be described in terms of axis rotations. Sometimes, unconstrained objects will rotate about a fixed axis. Sometimes, the axis of rotation will wobble slightly. Sometimes, it moves around wildly. Merely watching objects tossed into the air and redescribing their movement in terms of axis rotations can be an excellent exercise in empiricism and redescription.

The question of how one represents rotations by numbers can be raised explicitly. The standard method of using a vector pointing along the axis of rotation whose length is proportional to speed of rotation is only one possibility. The reason why it is universally used is that it has one fundamentally nice property: Two simultaneous rotations (which can be modeled as a program alternating small periods of the different rotations) produce a net rotation that corresponds to the sum of the vectors representing the two combined rotations. That it does can be proved using simple geometry on the imagistic representation, picturing an object rotating about different axes. Thus, one makes a fundamental epistemological point. Mathematical formalisms can be invented and shaped to a task, but they must be interpreted, and they have their final justification only in capturing in a simply manipulable way some essential features of the physical thing, attribute, or operation that they represent.

References

Abelson, H., and diSessa, A. *Report on an NSF Student Science Training Program in Physics, Mathematics and Computer Science.* Technical Report 393. Cambridge, Mass.: Artificial Intelligence Laboratory, Massachusetts Institute of Technology, 1976.

Abelson, H., and diSessa, A. A. *Turtle Geometry: The Computer as a Medium for Exploiting Mathematics.* Cambridge, Mass.: M.I.T. Press, 1981.

Commission on Precollege Education in Mathematics, Science, and Technology. *Educating Americans for the Twenty-First Century.* Washington, D.C.: National Science Board, 1983.

diSessa, A. A. "On Learnable Representations of Knowledge." In J. Lochhead and J. Clement (Eds.), *Cognitive Process Instruction.* Philadelphia: Franklin Institute Press, 1979.

diSessa, A. A. "Momentum Flow as an Alternative Perspective in Elementary Mechanics." *American Journal of Physics,* 1980, *48,* 365–369.

diSessa, A. A. *The Role of Experience in Models of the Physical World.* Proceedings of the 3rd annual conference of the Cognitive Science Society, Berkeley, Calif., August 1981.

diSessa, A. A. "Phenomenology and the Evolution of Intuition." In D. Gentner and A. Stevens (Eds.), *Mental Models.* Hillsdale, N.J.: Erlbaum, 1983.

diSessa, A. A., and Globerson, T. "The Effect of Age and Cognitive Style on Children's Intuitions of Motion." Paper presented at Logo 84, Cambridge, Mass., June 28, 1984.

Goldin, G. A. "Levels of Language in Mathematical Problem Solving." In J. C. Bergeron and N. Herscovics (Eds.), *Proceedings of the Fifth Annual Meeting of the International Group for Psychology of Mathematics Education.* Montreal: Department of Mathematics, Concordia University, 1983.

Kohlberg, L. "Development of Moral Character and Moral Ideology." *Review of Child Development Research,* 1964, *1,* 383–431.

Lakatos, I. *Proofs and Refutations.* New York: Cambridge University Press, 1976.

Larkin, J. H., Simon, D. P., and Simon, H. A. "Models of Competence in Solving Physics Problems." *Cognitive Science,* 1980, *4,* 317–345.

Miller, M. "A Structured Planning and Debugging Environment for Elementary Programming." *International Journal of Man-Machine Studies,* 1979, *11,* 79–95.

Newell, A., and Simon, H. A. *Human Problem Solving.* Englewood Cliffs, N.J.: Prentice-Hall, 1972.

Papert, S. *Mindstorms: Children, Computers, and Powerful Ideas.* New York: Basic Books, 1980.

Pea, R. D. "What Is Planning Development the Development of?" In D. L. Forbes and M. T. Greenberg (Eds.), *Children's Planning Strategies.* New Directions for Child Development, no. 18. San Francisco: Jossey-Bass, 1982.

124

Perry, W. B. *Forms of Intellectual and Ethical Development in the College Years: A Scheme.* New York: Holt, Rinehart and Winston, 1970.

Polya, G. *How to Solve It.* Princeton, N.J.: Princeton University Press, 1945.

Rubinstein, M. F. "A Decade of Experience in Teaching an Interdisciplinary Problem-Solving Course." In D. T. Tuma and F. Reif (Eds.), *Problem Solving and Education: Issues in Teaching and Research.* Hillsdale, N.J.: Erlbaum, 1980.

Schoenfeld, A. "Teaching Problem-Solving Skills." *American Mathematical Monthly,* 1980, *87* (10), 794–805.

Tuma, D. T., and Reif, F. (Eds.). *Problem Solving and Education: Issues in Teaching and Research.* Hillsdale, N.J.: Erlbaum, 1980.

Wickelgren, W. *How to Solve Problems.* San Francisco: W. H. Freeman, 1974.

Andrea A. diSessa is senior scientist in the M.I.T. Laboratory for Computer Science, where he directs the Educational Computing Group.

Index

A

Abelson, H., 114, 115, 123
Abelson, R., 37, 53
Acker, S., 55n, 64, 71, 72
ACM, 77–78
Action trails, 14–15, 22–24, 62
American Educational Research Association, 1
Anderson, J. H., 17
Anderson, J. R., 78, 83, 94
Animated cartoons, 24–26
Arons, A. B., 93
Artificial intelligence (AI) systems, 81–82, 83, 88, 90, 93
AtariLab, Temperature Module of, 29

B

Baggett, P., 63, 71
Baker, P., 55n
Balanchine, G., 59, 71
Bamberger, J., 71
Bank Street Writer, 1
Barker, C, 72
Barr, A., 76, 93–94
BASIC, 61
Beach, R., 50, 52
Bennette, J., 93
Bertoff, A., 52
Block, J. H., 17
Block play simulation, 32–33
Boden, M. A., 86–87, 94
Bork, A., 57, 71
Boyer, C. B., 21, 34
Boyle, C. F., 78, 83, 94
Bransford, J. D., 94
Brown, A. L., 82, 83, 87, 94, 95
Brown, J. S., 77, 83, 85, 86, 94, 96
Bruner, J. S., 63, 72, 80, 90, 94, 95
Buchanan, B. G., 95
Burton, R., 77, 94

C

Cambre, M., 57–58, 71
Campione, J. C., 94
Caramazza, A., 18
Carbonell, J. G., 95
Carey, S., 82, 87, 94
Case, R., 79, 87, 94
Cazden, C., 43, 52
Chaillé, C., 1, 5–18, 55, 62
Champagne, A. B., 8, 17
Char, C., 63, 71, 72
Chatman, S., 63, 71
Chen, M., 8, 18
Cherry, R., 52
Children: computer graphics for, 19–35; and computer information-processing systems, 87–88; disabled, 16; and expert systems, 77; and intuitive epistemology, 108–109; physical knowledge acquisition by, 9–12; symbolic development of, 20; theory building by, 5–18
Children's development: at one and one-and-a-half years, 20; at eleven through fifteen yeras, 40–51
CHOREO, 58–59
Clancey, W., 93
Cognitive trace systems, pedagogic, 85–87
Coleco Industries, Smurf Paint and Play Workshop by, 25–26, 61
Collins, A., 83, 93, 94, 96
Commission on Precollege Education in Mathematics, Science, and Technology, 98, 123
Computer graphics: analysis of value of, 19–35; examples of, 21–33; features of, 19–20; for imagery assessing, 64–70; and interaction, 62, 69; tools and techniques of, 61–62; uses of, 57–59; for visual imagery and spatial thought, 55–73
Computers: classroom put into, 29; and development, 37–38, 55–56, 83–92; for editing of writing, 37–53; as enhancer and illustrator, 57–62; and epistemology, 98, 111, 114–117, 119; human intelligence system integrated with, 75–96; information processing by, and children, 87–88; medium of,

D. Cicchetti, K. Schneider-Rosen (Eds.), *Childhood Depression.*
New Directions for Child Development, no. 26, December 1984.

ERRATA

Page 67, line 8:

The number .1110 should reach .0001

Page 72, Table 3, first center column heading should read:

Psychosocial Symptoms

T. H. Carr (Ed.), *The Development of Reading Skills.*
New Directions for Child Development, no. 27, March 1985.

ERRATA

On page 68 in the paper by Bock and Br͟͟͟͟͟͟͟͟͟͟ occurrences of
"Johnson and Barrett" should be replaced by "Johnson and Smith." The
reference list on page 73 should include the following citation:

Johnson H., and Smith, L. B. "Children's Inferential Abilities in the Context of Reading to Understand." *Child Development,* 1981, *52,* 1216–1223.